BEACH BOATS
OF BRITAIN

Suffolk beach punt *Alice Maud*, built 1884 and out of register in 1966, running summer pleasure trips   (Dunwich Museum)

BEACH BOATS
OF BRITAIN

Robert Simper

THE BOYDELL PRESS · WOODBRIDGE

© Robert Simper 1984

First published 1984
The Boydell Press Ltd.
P.O. Box 9, Woodbridge,
Suffolk IP12 3DF

British Library Cataloguing in Publication Data

Simper, Robert
  Beach boats of Britain.
  1. Boats and boating — Great Britain — History
  I. Title
  623.8'29   VM351

ISBN 0 85115 195 7

Printed in Great Britain by
St Edmundsbury Press, Bury St Edmunds, Suffolk

Contents

Acknowledgements

The material for this book has been gathered by reading up the written accounts of beach boats and then talking to the fishermen and residents at as many places as possible. Although I have done a great deal of travelling, this work would still not have been completed without good local knowledge. In the north-east of England, George Stanton, Hector Handyside and A. Goodall aided the recording of fishing and building cobles. On the East Anglian coast many have helped, including John Perryman, John Winter, Billy English, John and Doreen Cragie, Billy Burrel, Dick Harman, Mick Lynn, Colin Fox, George Jago and Charlie Brinkley.

In the Thanet area, Hugh Perks put me in contact with V. E. Kennard, while at Deal Mrs Will Honey kindly allowed me to use her late husband's photograph collection. On the south coast, A. Clements of Dungeness and Steven Peak were very informative about the boats on that coast. Hilton Matthews acted as guide on the Isle of Wight and introduced me to Andy Butler and Jim Richards. From Devon, Charles Easterbrook supplied me with local knowledge and John McDonald of the Falmouth Working Boat Association went to much trouble to find information about the Cornish landings. On the Isles of Scilly, I talked to Alf Jenkins, Brian Jenkins and Tom Chudleigh about gigs.

From Wales Dr J. Geraint Jenkins of the Welsh Industrial and Maritime Museum made his research into the Welsh herring fishing available. Peter and Edna Barton made research in North Wales and the Mersey area much easier. Alan Lockett's books proved a useful guide to the Morecambe Bay area and here Tom Smith talked about his fishing. Richard Langhorne of Lancashire County Museum Service helped with locating photographs.

From West Scotland Jeremy Cresswell helped while Angus Martin generously made his researches into local fishing methods available. On the east coast of Scotland J. Hobson Rankin of the Scottish Veteran & Vintage Fishing Vessel Club introduced me to Rod McMillian of Broughty Ferry and Gillian Zealand of Arbroath Museum, as well as generally aiding my research. In Shetland, A. Williamson of Shetland Museum took a great deal of trouble to get the facts correct and Tom Moncrieff and Joe and Hazel Grey also aided the search for the forgotten era of the *haaf* inshore fishing. From Northern Ireland Michael McCaughan of the Ulster Folk & Transport Museum made much of his original material available.

On inshore fishing generally thanks go to Paddy O'Driscoll and the Editor of Fishing News, on the photographic side thanks to Ron van den Bos and Geoff Cordy; while my wife Pearl has been responsible for the typing and marathon task of indexing. Thanks must go to my son Jonathan for his continued enthusiasm in beach boats.

Robert Simper
Ramsholt, 1984

Chapter 1
Living Through the Surf

The noise of the sea breaking as it meets the land is the dominating sound on every beach. That sound marks the dividing line between man's natural element, dry land, and the inhospitable open sea. In a gale, the breaking seas make a roar which leaves no doubt as to the danger they present. Even in calm weather the sea is never wholly still and there is always a faint murmur at the water's edge. For centuries men have felt the need and the challenge to go through the barrier of surf and breakers and out on the restless sea.

It is most probable that in the British Isles men first ventured off the beach in simple dug-out canoes or skin boats. It would seem that they found skin boats the most effective, because when Julius Caesar first landed in south east England in 55 BC he recorded that the local people used these. Boats made from a framework of tree branches covered with animal skins could be made with a few very simple tools, but they were still capable of making sea voyages. No doubt the Romans, when they occupied Britain, encouraged shipbuilding in wood, but three hundred years after Julius Caesar, another Roman writer recorded that skin boats were used for trade between Britain and Ireland.

It is doubtful if skin boats were widely used in Britain much after the Roman period, although some historians believe that the coble of the north east coast of England was developed from skin boats. The fact that skin boats have been in regular commercial use on freshwater rivers right into modern times, proves that they were a practical form of transport. The round wicker coracles give an idea of what form the early craft might have taken. Coracles have been declining, not because a better technique has been found for river boats, but because angling interests have been suppressing surface drift netting for salmon. The coracle was used on isolated rivers in Scotland until the 1890s. The Elgin Museum have a coracle which was used on the River Spey until this period. In England, far inland, in what was the county of Shropshire, and is now Salop, coracle fishing went on normally until the 1930s. In 1980 Eustace Rogers of Ironbridge was the last of the English traditional coracle builders still at work, although happily other people have learnt the art to continue it. Wales remains the stronghold of the coracle although even here the anglers have slowly driven them out. No coracles are left operating in north Wales and only a few remain in southern Wales.

The only area in the British Isles where skin boats still work off open beaches is the west coast of Ireland. The use of skin boats or currachs is mentioned in Irish mythology and in the records of Irish monks as early as 500 AD. This legend and accounts have been interpreted to mean that the Celtic people reached north America before the Vikings. That could be true, but there is no real evidence of an Atlantic crossing. However there is absolutely no doubt that skin boats from Ireland were making long voyages in north-west Europe between the fourth and sixth centuries.

After this the plank boat was being widely adopted. The currachs were pushed back to the fresh water rivers of eastern Ireland, from where they dropped out of use early this century, and to the west coast. This area has few trees so it made sense to keep to a skin boat. Besides, the currachs are cheap to build and light to carry up a beach.

The Gaelic for currach is *naomhog*, pronounced 'na vog', which is best translated as canoe. In a way they are more canoe than boat with the light timber framework covered by canvas (hide went out of use in the mid nineteenth century). The currachs of western Ireland are long and narrow and rely on their buoyant hulls to survive on the huge Atlantic swell. Most of the currachs are about 18ft long and can be rowed by two men.

The 75ft Oseberg longship is believed to have only been a coastal vessel. With the Gokstad and Tune longships she is housed in the Viking Museum, Oslo   (Author)

The larger 25ft currachs of the Dingle peninsula usually need four men, but can carry up to two tons. The bows rake upwards to lift on the Atlantic seas while the sterns are square and shallow for easy beaching. The currachs are rowed with flat oars on a single throle, but the larger ones of Aran and county Kerry used to have low lug sails, now replaced by outboards.

Just about every place within reach of water in the counties of Donegal, Mayo and Connemara had currachs, but they did not spread south into the Dingle peninsula in county Kerry until about 1850 and they even took a few decades more to be adopted in the Basket Islands. In this century the Aran Islands out in the Atlantic became the great stronghold of the currach. They were used in great numbers for fishing and inter-island traffic. On the Aran islands of Inisheer and Inishmaan there were no piers so when the steamers arrived everything had to be brought ashore on to the beach by currach. Anyone wanting to go ashore had to bargain with the men for the trip. Cattle for shipment to the mainland were swum out astern of the currach with the men keeping their head above water and then they were hoisted up on the steamer's deck by derrick. All this kind of work called for highly seaworthy craft and even if a currach was damaged the repair to the skin was a simple operation, easily within the ability of men who earnt their living working with their hands.

In the 1950s when currachs were still being built in large numbers for £24 a hull, a new use was found for them. This was the rise in popularity of racing currachs under oar for pleasure. The first racing championship was held at Salt Hill near Galway in 1954 with races usually between four man currachs. The major event is the Dingle Regatta which has become a social event largely sponsored by Guinness, in which rival crews of different regions compete, watched by enthusiastic crowds. The currachs used for the regattas are sleeker and have less beam than the true beach craft and are known as 'racers' to distinguish them.

These sea-going currachs of Western Ireland are the last of the European skin boats. In Scandinavia rock carvings show that skin boats were in regular use there in the Bronze Age. Many (but not all) scholars believe that the double-ended skin boat propelled by paddles progressed on in the Iron Age to become planked double-ended boats. The 33ft Als Boat, found in a bog in southern Denmark in 1921, dates from about 300 BC and its features suggest the builder copied skin boats.

Another Danish bog, this time in Jutland, preserved the 73ft Nydam oak boat. She is believed to date from around 400 AD a time when the classic Viking longship was clearly emerging. This was the period of the great Continental migrations when Europe was starting to take political shape. The Sutton Hoo longship of 600 AD was excavated from burial mounds in 1939 on the Sutton Walks, a lonely stretch of heathland in Suffolk. In 1968 the site was reopened and although the actual ship had completely decayed away, it was possible to see its shape in the sand. It was the most curious hull shape I have ever seen. The hull of the Sutton Hoo ship must have been about 89ft long, but it was so beamy that she could have floated in just a few feet of water: a craft which could have landed on a beach anywhere or be pushed far inland up a river. Some scholars have suggested that she was not a seagoing craft, yet since the nearby River Deben is only about seven miles of navigable water, it is hard to believe that anyone would have built a ship of this size just to stay in the river.

   The Sutton Hoo Anglo-Saxon ship belongs to the Migration Period and it was during
the later Viking Age that true Norse longships reached their perfection. Less is known
about the round ship or knorr, in which the Viking merchants carried cargoes and made
Atlantic voyages. The longship was the secret weapon with which the Vikings almost
destroyed Christianity. The first record of a raid in England by Vikings was in 793 when
they looted the Lindisfarne monastery on Holy Island. For the next two centuries no
part of the British Isles was ever safe from a sudden raid by Vikings. The Norse pirates
used longships which must have been very similar to the Gokstad ship of about AD 900
which is on display at the Viking Ship Hall at Bygdoy in Oslo.
   The Gokstad longship represents a piece of technology every bit as politically
devastating as the hydrogen bomb. The Anglo-Saxon Christians believed, at least to start

with, in peace, and thought that if they offered no resistance the warlike Vikings would be won over to their way of thinking. They could not have been more wrong. The Vikings took this as a sign of weakness and looted and settled Northern Europe as they felt inclined. The rest of Europe had not got ships capable of going to raid Scandinavia. It was only when Christian kings and chiefs fought back and beat the Vikings in battle that the Norse aggression was finally overcome and the people of Scandinavia in turn adopted Christianity.

The Viking longship was designed to go anywhere and land anywhere, but when the Viking Age finished the story of British beach boats began. After the Viking Age boats were built to land on just one beach. Builders had to produce, not a general purpose troopship-cum-battleship, but a boat type for just one set of purely local conditions. The definition of a traditional craft is one which is designed, built and used in just one community or one section of a coastal area. Traditional craft were seldom completely static in design. As new fishing methods or a new type of work appeared, then the local boat types were altered to suit the latest needs. We can be fairly certain that working conditions throughout the medieval period (and indeed long after) did not alter a great deal. In Norway small boat types in some areas stayed almost identical for a thousand years, because the small open boats found buried with the Gokstad ship were very similar to those built for everyday use until well after World War II. In Britain boat types have retained some Norse features, but generally speaking changes in maritime technology increased efficiency in boat design by the eighteenth century. Although many beach landings were very isolated communities, many new ideas in hull design and sail plan were brought home by men who had served in the Royal and Merchant Navies and were adopted into the local tradition.

The very term beach boat must cover any craft which has operated off any open beach. Generally speaking beach boats are hauled out of the water at the end of the working day, but there are no hard and fast rules. Every beach landing is different; that is why each type of boat is unique to that one place. Often one boat type, such as the coble on the north-east coast of England, will cover a long stretch of the coast, but there are always local differences.

To understand just how each type of beach boat evolved, one has to go into the social background and local conditions of each beach landing to see how certain traditions grew. Every place has its highly intriguing story. Each individual boat is a combination of at least two ideas: the man who ordered the boat gave instructions as to what he required, and the boatbuilder who used the experience he carried in his head, produced craft developed from some that he had already built.

From medieval times onwards harbours were being built around Britain either by dredging river mouths or building piers on open coasts. The creation of man-made harbours was particularly common on the rocky coasts of Cornwall and Eastern Scotland. Here many beach landings became harbours by the construction of stone piers, but it was impossible to do this on a coast where the soil crumbled away. This is why beach landings survived in larger numbers in East Anglia and along the coast of southern England. The other great stronghold of beach boats, the north-east of England, did have rocks, but there continued to be problems with erosion there and often the small number of boats at each landing failed to produce enough revenue to construct a harbour.

Yorkshire cobles on the Seaton Garth landing at Staithes in about 1900. The coble was evolved for working off open beaches from a combination of skin boats and the Norse boatbuilding tradition   (Bowes Museum)

On any part of the coast which did not have a harbour, natural or man-made, men were forced to work off open beaches. There was plenty of work – fishing, pilotage, salvage and cargo handling – done from open beaches, to say nothing of a long period of highly organized smuggling around 1800. From the Viking Age until the end of the eighteenth century there is remarkably little accurate pictorial or written evidence about the beach boats. Nor have any true beach boats survived from this period, but there are some similar craft from the late eighteenth century still in existence which give a general idea. One is the 25ft open schooner yacht *Peggy* built in 1791 on the Isle of Man. She was later bricked up in her boathouse at Castletown, which is now part of a maritime museum. In the Lake District at the Windermere Steamboat Museum there is a lug sail boat of 1780 and parts of another boat believed to date from 1735.

These craft show quite clearly that in the eighteenth century boat building in wood was a highly developed craft and most builders could turn out anything that beachmen ordered. That is exactly what happened because in the nineteenth century a profusion of widely different traditional boat types appeared all over Britain. The vast majority of traditional beach boats were open and seldom exceeded 25ft in length. There were some larger craft, up to about 60ft in the case of the East Anglian salvage yawls, and some decked boats operated on the south coast of England. Across the North Sea in the Netherlands, on the long sandy coast of Zuid and Noord Holland, where there were no

7

Suffolk longline fishermen at Dunwich, November 1983   (East Anglian Daily Times)

natural harbours, the 'bomshuit' were their decked craft which were capable of staying at sea for many days on a herring voyage. There were smaller but similar craft along the coast of Belgium and northern France, but getting them in and out of the water was a major operation and they dropped out of favour once the harbours were built.

Beach boats reached their peak in numbers in Britain in the mid nineteenth century. During that century the population was growing at a tremendous rate and there must have been many thousands of men earning a living working boats off open beaches. This reached its height in about 1890 when there were over 350 places around the coast of Britain which were beach landings of some description. After this, beach landings steadily declined until World War I: and then commercial activity off beaches declined until World War II. However, in the decades since then, the use of beach boats for full or part time longshore fishing and recreation boating has been steadily increasing. There are still about a hundred beach landings in Britain where men work boats for a living. However, it is a bit difficult to be dogmatic about numbers, because although there is no doubt that beach landings like Filey, Aldeburgh and Hastings are commercial centres, there are other places where just one or a few boats work in local fishing seasons. Very often men rely on some other form of income (including state benefit) for much of the year.

8

A survey of beach landings round the coast of Britain is a fascinating subject because of the tremendous variety of craft. Beach boats must be the oldest form of working craft in regular use. For centuries they have been the backbone and life blood of countless small communities around Britain. The central feature of many beach landings in the past one and a half centuries has usually been the lifeboat. However, the story of the life-saving society's rescue work, although it brings out some of the better qualities in the human race, is outside this survey, which concentrates on commercial craft.

At some point in history just about every beach in Britain has been a landing place. Every part of Britain still has commercial craft working off open beaches. It is only when (as I did) one goes out and attempts to make a survey of beach landings that one realises just how many hundreds of places are still beach landings. Behind virtually every sheltered headland there is nearly always a little group of boats hauled up. Each place has its own highly individual story.

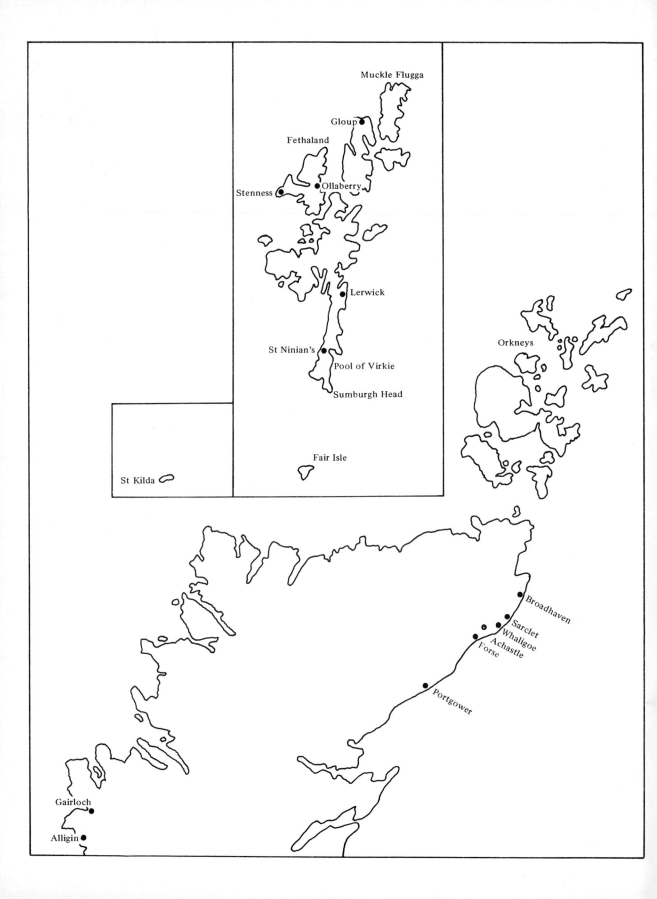

Muckle Flugga

Gloup

Fethaland

Ollaberry

Stenness

Lerwick

St Ninian's

Pool of Virkie

Sumburgh Head

Orkneys

Fair Isle

St Kilda

Broadhaven

Sarclet

Whaligoe

Achastle

Forse

Portgower

Gairloch

Alligin

Chapter 2
Norse Legacy

Even by the standards of the Shetland Isles Stenness is now a remote place. It is just a hamlet of crofts by a small sheltered inlet on the Atlantic coast. Around the beach at the head of Stenness Sound are some ruined stone buildings. Only sheep graze there now, but until the last decade of the nineteenth century these were the store, salt cellar, shop and lodges which made a *haaf* fishing station. In Shetlandic, *haaf* means ocean and the *haaf* fishery meant literally ocean fishing. Stenness and about fifty other similar places were bases or landing stations for men who went out after ling and cod into the Atlantic up to the edge of the continental shelf.

No one is certain when the *haaf* fishing started although Shetland boats caught mainly ling and cod for sale to the Hanse merchants possibly as early as the fourteenth and fifteenth centuries. Scarcity of these species on the nearer grounds, possibly caused by a combination of overfishing and changing conditions of sea temperatures and ocean currents caused the greater concentration on the far *haaf* grounds. This was one cause of the development of bigger boats, known as the sixareen or sixern. It is certain that the men of Shetland had a tradition stretching right back to the Vikings of going to sea in small boats. To the Norse seafarer, Shetland was the crossroads. The Vikings came either on passage to Scotland or when bound westward to the Faroes, Iceland, Greenland and even the North American continent.

Shetland, together with the Orkneys and Caithness, the most northern part of Scotland, were Norse territory from the ninth century AD and never part of Gaelic Scotland. In England and Lowland Scotland the Scandinavian influence ended abruptly with the victory of William, Duke of Normandy at the Battle of Hastings in 1066. The Norse influence held out in Shetland until 1469 when a Danish king pledged Shetland to the King of Scotland as part of a payment of a dowry of a Danish princess. Shetland was left to its own devices and the only real economy it could develop was selling dried fish. Most of the trade went through the Norwegian port of Bergen and other Hanseatic ports, but it was controlled by German merchants. This lasted until the eighteenth century when Shetland merchants gained control, but the connection with Bergen remained.

Until the second half of the nineteenth century the lairds, most of whom were descended from men from Scotland, dominated Shetland. The lairds acted as merchants and forced the fishermen-crofters to sell all their produce from sea and land to them under threat of eviction from their crofts. Very little money ever changed hands as the merchants-lairds supplied goods in return. Given the rather medieval economic conditions of Shetland this style was as good as any. Indeed in the hands of the honest landowner it worked well enough, but in the hands of the unscrupulous landlord it meant that crofters became little more than serfs. This 'truck' system of payment, where prices were set by merchants, resulted in the fishermen-crofters being permanently in debt to the landlord.

The men worked on their crofts in the winter, which gave them food and clothing, but in order to earn more they left their families to look after the crofts in the summer and went to the *haaf*. The fish landing stations were all situated on the coast as near to the rich fishing grounds as possible; but to reach these grounds the men had to go out into the open Atlantic for several days at a time.

Since Shetland has very few trees, the boats used were imported from Norway. The main area supplying them was around Hardanger Fjord until the last decades of the nineteenth century. It is asssumed that the boats imported as hulls or in kit form would have been similar to the Norwegian boats although references to 'Shetland boats' in Norwegian regional administrative records suggest in 1836 that boats were built specially for the conditions in Shetland. Although trade with Britain had been slowly increasing over the centuries, the first regular link with Britain came in 1840 when a summer steamer service was established. However, timber imports continued to come mainly from Scandinavia and the Baltic ports. The *haaf* fishing was also expanding, so the need for more boats prompted the growth of boat building in Shetland and by 1860 most of the craft were built in the islands from imported timber.

In the 1840s some nine thousand men and boys were working at the *haaf* and it was the main economy of Shetland. However, it was still organised and carried out in a way that the Vikings would have clearly understood. The boats were the most important tool at the *haaf*. In most British beach landings the type of boats used were based on the Norse double ender, but as the centuries passed these were adapted for coming ashore in the local conditions. In Shetland they remained closer to the Norse original, partly through the continual contact with Norway, but mainly because the conditions in Shetland were so rugged that none of the Norse seakeeping qualities in the hull could be sacrificed for the convenience of a hull more easily landed and hauled up the beach. The larger boats were sometimes anchored in the sheltered voes and bays between fishing.

In Norway eight-twelve oared boats were used in the offshore fishery, but in Shetland, boats of about 30ft overall pulled by six oars were used. It was the use of six oars which gave them the name 'sixern'. These could be both rowed and sailed, the sail being a simple squaresail which had to be lowered on each tack, but the procedure was different from an ordinary dipping lug. With the true Norse square sail it could be swung round the mast, but with the higher peaked sail used on the sixern this was not possible.

In a working week during the summer *haaf* the fishermen tried to make two trips and return home on Sundays. While at sea they frequently only had an oatmeal bread with 'bland' for a drink. This was thin milk left over from cheese making and was considered

Sixerns at the Shetland *haaf* fishing station of Fethaland in about 1895   (Shetland Museum)

to be very thirst-quenching. They carried other food also, and when possible they lit a fire of peats in a fire kettle and did some rudimentary cooking or at least brewed a hot drink. Between hauling by hand and resetting the seven miles of long line each sixern carried, the men occasionally 'rolled themselves up in the sail' in the foreroom of the boat and had a quick nap, for on a good trip they sometimes hauled up to two tons of fish.

If the weather seemed to be turning bad then they hauled their lines and made for shelter. However, even though the sixerns were superb sea boats most summers saw some of them overwhelmed by sudden gales. A diary by Christopher Sanderson written between 1824–90 records two tragedies at Stenness. In 1830 the diary records: 'Andrew Williamson's boat was swamped coming in from the *haaf* yesterday, himself and three others drowned. Wm Bigland's boat had not come in and there is little hope of them.' Three days later a third sixern had not returned and had been given up as being lost.

Stenness had twenty-nine sixerns at this period and was one of the larger *haaf* stations. There were at least fifty other stations operating around the Isles of Shetland at that time. The greatest *haaf* disaster was in 1832 when no less than thirty-two sixerns were lost in a single NNW gale. Some of the men from these were saved but 105 men and boys lost their lives.

During the night of 20–21 July 1881 a sudden and terrible gale caught most of the *haaf* fishermen at sea on the far grounds. In that single night fifty-eight men were lost leaving thirty-four widows and eighty-five children. The worst hit station in this disaster was Gloup, North Yell.

13

The abandoned *haaf* fishing station of Stenness on Mainland Shetland. The central boat is a Shetland Model with flat oars worked on a single throle   (Author)

The men of Gloup had not been off for several days and at 5 a.m. had met on the beach to decide what to do. It was hazy, the sea was smooth, but there was a considerable westerly swell coming in. This swell worried the older men who fretted that the weather had not yet settled down; however, everyone was anxious to get to sea to go fishing and twenty-six sixerns set out. Many hours later the sky to the north looked very black and foreboding, and not long afterwards the men heard the roar of approaching wind and could see the water turning white as it came down from the East by North. The fishermen were used to being out in bad weather and started to haul their lines, planning to use the ling as ballast and to pay for their day at sea.

Most of the boats were between forty to fifty miles off the narrow entrance to Gloup Voe. It called for considerable skill in navigation just to find their voe in the rapidly deteriorating conditions and in the early hours of the morning most of the sixerns came in safely, although several had near misses. All these were boats which had been in the water around Muckle Flugga, the most northerly point of Shetland. Others which had gone out westward could not sail eastward enough against the gale to reach the mouth of Gloup Voe. To westward of Gloup, the coast of Yell is sheer cliff with no haven. Three of the six sixerns lost were driven on to this coast. It must have been terrible to have heard the roar of the seas on the cliff approaching and to have known that there was no hope. One sixern was seen coming into Gloup Voe, but just off the entrance the

14

sail suddenly dropped, perhaps the halyard broke, at any rate the sixern rolled over instantly and was gone for ever. Another sixern tried to make for the safety of Westing, Unst, and was swamped while trying to find a landing and a third was probably swamped at sea.

All these were lost on approaching land, but the smallest Gloup sixern, the *Water Witch*, had survived by staying at sea with her crew rowing her head to sea. The large boats were too heavy for the men to row head to sea for hours on end. The surprising thing about the night of the 'Gloup disaster' was not that ten boats and all their crews were lost, but that so many small open boats survived out in the open Atlantic in the full fury of a gale and in the truly terrible waves.

When caught in a gale a sixern's skipper and crew had to decide whether to run before the gale and risk being overwhelmed by the sea, or to make for the *haaf* station beach and risk being swamped going ashore. Staying at sea was usually recognised to be safer but much harder on the men. When sailing in a gale the practice was to have two men on the halyard, one hauling the sail up and one hauling the sail down. In the troughs between the seas the sail was hoisted, but on going up on the wave crest into the full force of the gale, the sail was dropped. Even in the troughs, care had to be taken not to get back wind (backflann) in the sixern's single square sail. If this happened the sail had to be lowered instantly so that the sixern did not capsize. Another precaution was that one man always held the mainsheet and this was never made fast so that it could always be released in a squall. The skipper sat in the aft compartment and steered with his shoulders on the tiller while the others bailed the water out when necessary.

The Shetland men spoke of being able 'to run a sea down' which meant manoeuvring the boat among the crests so that the seas were allowed to overtake the boat at their lowest and weakest part, away from the breaking crests. The boat would run along through the trough of the sea until a suitable spot was reached and then the helm was put up and the boat brought directly stern on to the overtaking sea. This was when the sixern's sharp Norse-style stern came into its own. In gale conditions sixerns could make nine knots and could reach a state known as 'sea loose' when the air travelling under the hull tended to lift them up. When this happened the hull quivered and there was a sound like the hull being dragged over pebbles on a beach.

The *haaf* fishery was a hard and dangerous one, made worse by the exceptionally poor financial rewards. In 1881 an Act of Parliament finally freed the fishermen-crofters from servitude to the lairds which allowed the crofters to widen their horizons. Since the middle of the eighteenth century Shetland smacks had been gradually going further over the North Atlantic. Shetland smacks pioneered cod fishing in the Davis Straits and were no strangers to the Nord Kap of Norway. The Shetlanders turned away from the *haaf* and developed an offshore fishing fleet because it gave them a better income. The *haaf* stations were being abandoned through the 1890s and the last to close was Fethaland in about 1903. Some eighty years later it was still possible to see the ruined *haaf* station at Fethaland although it was still a couple of miles from the nearest road.

Other reminders are scarce. At Ollaberry on Yell Sound in the centre of Shetland there are traces of sixern 'noosts'. These noosts were boat shaped pits along the foreshore where the sixerns were stored in the winter to protect them from the high winds.

The practice of keeping boats in noosts is still common in Shetland. In the early 1980s most of the small townships of crofts grouped around sheltered inlets had a few 'Shetland model' boats hauled up in noosts although they were outnumbered by the ordinary GRP and wooden boats hauled up on the foreshore. The term Shetland model appears to mean the Shetland type. When the sixern, fourern (four oared boat which did not go out as far as the sixern) and the haddock boats (smaller version of the sixern used for inshore fishing in the winter) were replaced by the 'long boom' smacks, the Shetlanders still preferred to have smaller versions of the old offshore types for general purpose because they were so much more handy.

The Shetland model clearly shows its ancient Norse origin, but it was also the product of competitive racing. In 1809 an observer wrote rather begrudgingly about the waste of time caused by the sixerns all racing out to the grounds. The men from a *haaf* station all waited and set out at the same time in order to have a race, which must no doubt have made their working lives more interesting. Since small boats were the main form of passenger transport between the islands, speed was always important. Informal racing was called 'kemping' and had long been a favourable past time in Shetland when in the mid-Victorian period, organized yacht racing was started.

The Lerwick Boating Club was formed in 1880 with the object of promoting and developing the Shetland model. Although other forms of racing are now in the club's activities, races for the Shetland models are still its prime function. The desire for faster boats has seen the hulls being built narrower. There has also been a gradual updating of the rig. By the 1920s the racing Shetland models like the *Ripple* were being given a gunter sloop rig. The models were racing at Lerwick with a gunter until 1968 when *Arctic Mist* was given a second hand Flying Fifteen sail and her success led to other boats following suit. However, a popular event in the Lerwick Interclub Regatta, when the men from other islands bring Shetland models down to race, is the Square Sail Race. The men of Whalsay are particularly agile when lowering the squaresail and rehoisting it on the other side of the mast when tacking, as the sixerns had to do when fishing.

Down at the southern end of the Shetland archipeligo on the southern part of Mainland is the last true link with Norway, in the form of the Ness yoal. The Ness yoal is a narrow double ended pulling boat of about 20ft in length overall, and very light. This is the oldest of the Shetland types and was once common throughout the islands, but after the expansion of the *haaf* they were only used in Dunrossness. The yoal was particularly suited for saithe (coalfish) fishing. The saithe liked the strong tidal conditions caused by the Atlantic tide stream having to push through round the south of the Mainland. The men went out in yoals south of Sumburgh Head and rowed at speed, towing feathered or baited hooks in the water, which the fish grabbed.

There is a feeling of being very close to the Viking era in this part of Shetland. On nearby St Ninian's a great hoard of silver plate was found, probably buried by priests in terror of the approach of a Viking raiding party. At Sumburgh, there is Jarlshof, the remains of a Viking settlement. A few minutes' walk from Jarlshof at Grutness the Ness yoal *Viking* was still kept under the shelter of a wall in 1982. Her hull was very similar to the 'faring' (small boats) found with the ninth century Viking longship at Gokstad and now on display in Norway at the Viking Ship Hall in Oslo.

Within sight of the Viking's landing place is the Pool of Virkie, a cove where huge rollers come crashing in and there were two more Ness yoals here in 1982. All of these

The Ness Yoal *Ivy* coming alongside the herring boat *Queen Adelaide* for bait c.1924. The *Ivy* was fishing in strong tidal waters off Sumburgh Head, at the southern end of Shetland   (Shetland Museum)

were modern and relied on outboards, but abandoned behind a dyke (stone wall) in a dilapidated state, was the *Ivy*, a Ness yoal dating from before World War I. At Dunrossness Voe, I met Tom Moncrieff, the last person to work the *Maggie*, a Ness yoal built for his grandfather in 1901. On examining both *Ivy* and *Maggie* the overriding impression was of just how light and flexible they were. The hulls twisted as one lifted one side, which made them easier to drag up over the wooden or whalebone 'bars' called linns, at the end of the day. At sea it allowed them to be flexible in the motion of the sea so that the hull did not strain. The Vikings used this technique with their ocean going longships and both these and their tiny descendants, the Ness yoals, were fast under sail or oar. Tom Moncrief said: 'You could row a yoal all day and not get tired.' They just slipped through the water but the pointed stern made it difficult to fix an outboard. Most of the people in Dunrossness had gone over to a stronger transom-hulled boat for working lobster pots under power.

One cannot leave Shetland without mentioning another famous local boat type, the Fair Isle skiff. The Fair Isle is on its own about half way between Shetland and Orkney. There are no natural harbours although since World War II a small pier has been built. The Fair Isle skiffs were rowed by three men with a very fast chopping stroke which could get up to forty-five strokes a minute.

It is often said that the men of Shetland were fishermen who worked a croft, while the men of Orkney were crofters who owned a boat. Orkney is a great deal more fertile than much of Shetland and the men are naturally more concerned with farming. Being closer to the mainland resulted in the Orcadians developing their boats more on the lines of East Coast boats by the nineteenth century, rather than following the old Norse model.

The yoles of Orkney were primarily sailing craft used for fishing and inter-island ferries, and they did not go far off shore. The Orcadian yoles or jols were two-masted; those from the North Isles had lug sails while those from the South Isles were spritsail.

In the sparsely populated coast and islands of northern and western Scotland, a boat working from an open beach was a common form of transport. The Wick Society has acquired two yoles from Stroma, an island just off the north coast of Caithness. One of these, the 19ft *Miller* built in 1892, had also served as a sail boat to Eilean nan Ron (Seal Island), an island a little further along the coast. The *Miller* also took off the last inhabitants of Eilean nan Ron when the Island was evacuated in 1937. In 1984 the Wick Society completed restoring the scaffie *Spray* WK1767, built at Findochty in 1913, which is virtually the same size as the replica scaffie *Annie*.

Just about all the fishing on the East Coast of Scotland was conducted in open boats working off beaches until the early nineteenth century. Then the herring changed everything. The lairds started developing fishing villages and harbours in order to increase their rental income. The first priority of many a fishing community was to build

The Ness Yoal *Ivy* abandoned near the Pool of Virkie, Shetland in 1982. Of all the beach boats in the British Isles the Ness Yoal kept closest to the Viking traditions and were very lightly constructed with only five frames   (Author)

18

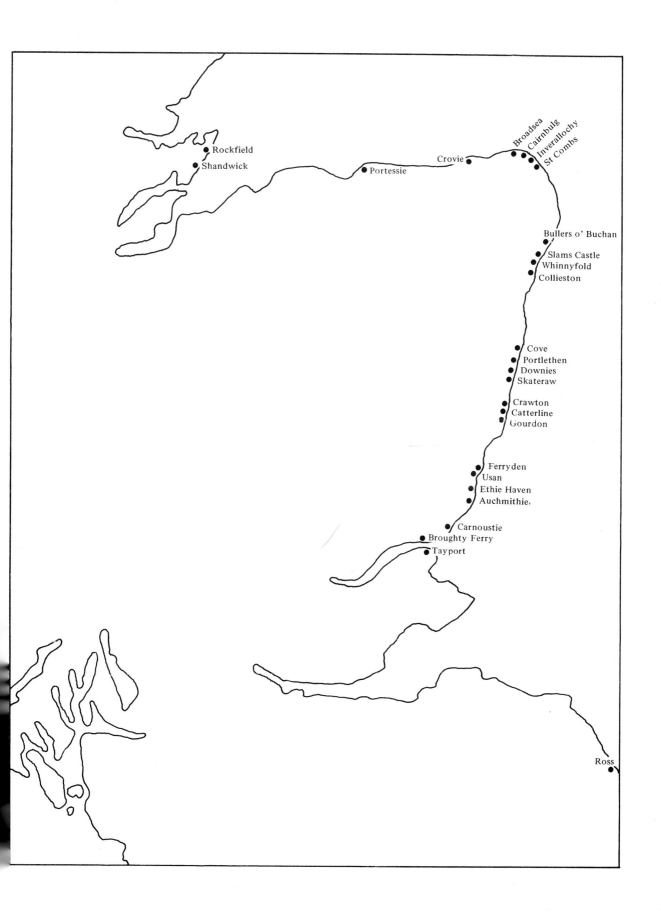

Rockfield
Shandwick
Portessie
Crovie
Broadsea
Cairnbulg
Inverallochy
St Combs
Bullers o' Buchan
Slams Castle
Whinnyfold
Collieston
Cove
Portlethen
Downies
Skateraw
Crawton
Catterline
Gourdon
Ferryden
Usan
Ethie Haven
Auchmithie,
Carnoustie
Broughty Ferry
Tayport
Ross

The *Annie*, sailed here as a yacht, is a replica of the 25ft scaffie *Gratitude* built in Banffshire in 1896. The square sail of the viking and medieval ships developed into the dipping lug sail. The lug sails closer to the wind, but has to be lowered and shifted round the mast on each tack   (Author)

a harbour. Once this had been achieved they could operate larger decked craft which generated enough income to expand the harbour. By 1900 there were very few beach landings left in Eastern Scotland; there were just a few small places where it was usually physically impossible to build a harbour.

Whaligoe on the south coast of Caithness is such a place. The landing is little more than a crack in the cliff face and the boats were hoisted out of the water by a derrick and lifted up on to a ledge. From here a stairway of some 365 steps twists its way up the cliff face. The women used to carry the fish in creels (baskets) on their backs up from the boats. The wives and daughters of the fishermen did much of the labouring side of the shore work. In the Moray Firth and further south this included carrying the men out through the water to their boats. The women folk, which included young girls, would 'kilt their coats' (tuck up their dress and petticoats) and wade bare footed out into the surf with the men on their backs. Of course the fishing communities were male dominated, but there was a practical reason for this custom. The men all wore leather thigh boots which, if dry, were warm; but they were not very water tight. To have gone off on a cold night with wet feet would have endangered their health. The women also came down in the morning to carry their men ashore, as drying leather boots in the tiny, already crowded, cottages would have been a problem.

20

The Montrose salmon fishermen. The men are wearing leather thigh boots   (Scottish Fisheries Museum)

Longshore fishing in the age of sail required the whole family to work. The men went to sea and looked after their boats, but the rest of the family spent their time mending nets, baiting great lines and generally fetching and carrying. Fishermen nearly always married fishermen's daughters so that they had someone who knew the work. In Scotland it was also the custom for women to manage the finances. This dates back to the time when fish wives walked round the district with baskets of fish on their backs hawking the days catch.

The women also did much of the work of curing the herring ashore. The curing yard was the focal point of all the herring harbours along the Scottish East Coast. It was the fact that the herring could be preserved in salt and did not have to be sold fresh that allowed this fishery to expand. In the late nineteenth century the herring fishery was reaching boom proportions and the 'fisher lassies' followed the fleet around the coast from Shetland to Yarmouth, curing the herring as it was landed.

Most of the fishing communities between the 'North Firth' (Moray Firth) and the 'South Firth' (Firth of Forth) managed to build some form of harbour in the nineteenth century. At Catterline, just south of Stonehaven on the Grampian coast, this amounted to just a short stone pier. There was too much swell coming in through the rocks for boats to lie against the tiny pier, but it offered protection to the beach landing. In the 1880s there were twenty-two boats working from Catterline; a few of these were large decked fifies, two-masted luggers, which followed the herring fleets from Shetland to Scarborough. At the end of the season these fifies were hauled ashore by a steam traction engine standing on the cliff top.

21

The ground to the north of the pier is now left empty, because when the steam drifters replaced sail, Catterline and many other small ports returned to local longshore fishing. The open boats were hauled ashore by a block and tackle, and when the women of the village saw the boats returning they walked down the cliff path and helped with the haul. Just after World War II there were still eight boats working from here, mainly crabbing, but the boats had to be hauled up from the tiny beach across the road by motor winch. In 1982 only the *Mascot* A440 remained working from Catterline.

Both Catterline and Auchmithie are small fishing villages perched on cliff tops. The fisherfolk of Auchmithie have over the centuries gradually moved to Arbroath, where the harbour was steadily improved. The plight of the poor people of Auchmithie became the concern of Annie Gilruth, a farmer's wife. Mrs Gilruth had gone to a great deal of effort to improve the school in the village and when she was told that the fishermen and their families would benefit from a harbour, she became the driving force behind the project. A small harbour was constructed at Auchmithie in about 1896, but it does not seem to have encouraged the growth of the local fishing fleet. A photograph of the

The fisher folk of Auchmithie with an open fifie. The long sweeps show that she relied on oar or sail for power. The fifie has a straight stern while the zulu had a raked stern   (Angus Museum)

A young girl at Auchmithie preparing flat fish for sale   (Angus Museum)

harbour in 1904 only shows four double-ended boats of the scaffie type. It would seem that the harbour never generated enough income to pay for its maintenance. By 1982 the harbour had gone, except that the foundation of the piers provided a little shelter for the pot boats landing at the bottom of the steep cliff.

In 1982 the fishery officer of this section of the coast said that he believed that although there were a great many unregistered boats, there were over 100 small boats between Dundee and Peterhead doing some commercial fishing off beaches. In the Arbroath district alone there were forty-eight salmon cobles. These had wide transom sterns off which the nets were paid out. The Scottish cobles are very beamy, to reduce the draught so that they can work in shallow water.

In the eighteenth century the landings at Fishtown of Usan, Ethie Haven and Auchmithie were all important fishing stations, but they remained just villages with a few boats working off the beach. South of Arbroath there were attempts to develop East Haven and West Haven, both beach landings on a rocky foreshore, as fishing stations. The Earl of Dalhousie built cottages in West Haven in the nineteenth century to encourage fishermen to work from here. The cottages at East Haven were also built by the laird to improve the rental value of the estate. In fact in Scotland the lairds did much to help (or in some cases hinder) the development of fishing.

East and West Haven are about two miles apart, but their histories are very similar. In 1856 there were nineteen boats working from here, mostly landing lobster which was collected by smack in the summer and taken to London. In the winter the West Haven men went long lining for cod which were salted down in barrels and sold abroad. The beach here is a fine sand and this attracted the railway company to create Carnoustie, a holiday resort which now engulfs West Haven. In 1982 East and West Haven had about five salmon cobles each and a few more pleasure boats kept on their beaches. To get the boats into the water they used 'jankes', trollies with boats slung underneath a frame.

Heading round Buddon Ness (the name Ness is of course Norse for a headland) one reaches Broughty Ferry, a pleasant suburb of Dundee overlooking the River Tay which once had a sizeable fleet of boats working off the beach. To say that Broughty Ferry was once a flourishing fishing centre would be incorrect, as the fisher folk here lived only slightly above subsistence level. In 1770 there were only a few fishermen's huts here and it would seem that salmon fishing in the Tay was their main occupation. This practice seems to have declined until about 1840, when the fishermen were going from the Tay to operate long lines in the open sea.

Most of the white fish landed were bought on the foreshore by 'cadgers' who then hawked them around Dundee. However when the railway arrived the practice changed and the fish were sent to Glasgow. The population of Broughty Ferry increased and the grey stone tenancy or 'lands' were built along the foreshore. A road runs along in front of these houses and it was no doubt to prevent the fishermen from blocking this right of way that the 'March stone' was erected beyond which boats were not allowed to be hauled up. The North British Railway Company built a small harbour at Broughty Ferry for the train ferry to cross to Tayport. This ferry stopped when the Tay bridge was built in 1877, but even with the harbour empty the fishermen still continued to use the beach probably because it was cheaper. By about 1880 there were 220 fishermen at Broughty Ferry operating around 80 boats. These had been bought secondhand from coastal fishing stations and only 23 were large enough to carry enough nets to go herring fishing.

Although Broughty Ferry had grown into a small town, this was largely due to the large families. Since so many fishermen had the same surname the use of bynames or nicknames was common. This was also a common practice at many other beach landings throughout Britain in the final decades of the era of sail.

In the late 1890s the Ferry ling fishermen began to find their grounds being ruined by the steam trawlers from the Firth of Forth and a few which were owned in Dundee. These Dundee trawlers were usually skippered and manned by the fishermen from the Ferry. The decline of Broughty Ferry as a fishing centre was hastened by social conditions ashore. The Ferry became an area where successful Dundee business men built spacious houses but the two communities, the rich manufacturers and the poor fisherfolk, never mixed. Indeed, the nannies to the children of the manufacturing families were told to cross the road if they saw any fisherfolk and not to let the children speak to them. It seems strange, at least to our modern thinking, that there was a total lack of resentment by the fisherfolk towards the rich; it was simply accepted that this was the order of things.

The lack of a middle class at Broughty Ferry during the Edwardian period probably hastened its decline as a fishing centre. There was a public enquiry into the problems at The Ferry, at which the fishermen spoke out against the conditions but there were no middle classes to organise better marketing or to campaign for the fishermen's cause.

Broughty Ferry had grown up as a river salmon fishing centre; then in Victorian times when this was exhausted the men turned to long lining at sea. However, Broughty Ferry is seven miles from the Tay Bar which is a particularly bad entrance. Faced with the distance and difficulties of reaching the fishing grounds The Ferry never really thrived. When, in the late nineteenth century, a tram system linking Dundee and Monifieth passed through the town, fishermen used it to get jobs in the jute and jam factories of Dundee.

Peter Anson, in his informative *Fishing Boats & Fisher Folk*, first published in 1930, refers to only twelve small boats at Broughty Ferry. Certainly the commercial fishing was on the verge of finishing and today there are no signs that it was a boat landing. Rod McMillian has recorded much of the town's past; and, as The Ferry had been a long lining centre, he went in 1979 to Gourdon, then one of the last places in Eastern

The fisher folk lived in real poverty before World War I. The women and children, barefoot, can be seen here at Broughty Ferry. In the background is a large open fifie   (Ron McMillian)

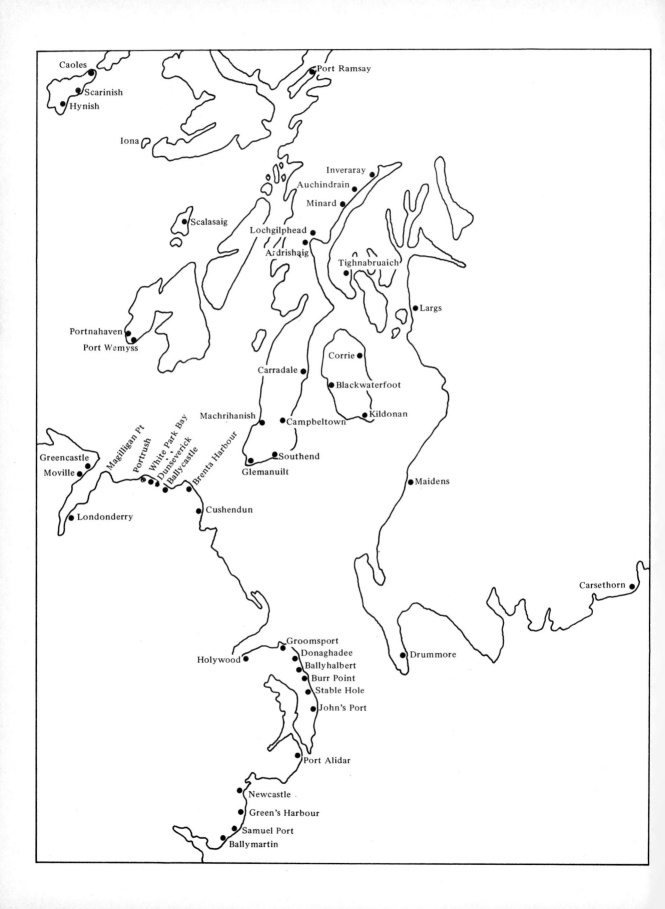

Scotland where long lines were used, to discover the methods used.

Each line was 300ft long with 100 'snoods' on which were three baited hooks. Each hook had to be baited individually. In the old days women had to go out and gather the limpets and mussels for bait, but in more recent times women only baited the lines. However, this was a very cold, monotonous task, and it looked as if long lining would finish at Gourdon because no one would do the baiting.

Leaving the east coast of Scotland, where there are only a few beach landings left, and crossing over the Lowlands to the Clyde, we find there were many craft working off open beaches. At Largs in 1895 there were about twenty 17ft line skiffs kept hauled up on the beach. These were a smaller version of the 30ft Loch Fyne skiffs, which were single-masted luggers with a very shallow forefoot under the bow and deep draught aft. This was evolved so that they could sit comfortably between posts facing up the beaches. These Loch Fyne skiffs were fast sailors, but being lightly built most had a short life. In 1972 the Auchindrain Museum of Country Life was given a 16ft upper Loch Fyne skiff which appears to have been a scaled down version of the Loch Fyne skiff and was probably built at Ardrishaig in about 1882 when herring fishing on the upper loch was at its height. She was fished from Minard and between Lochgilhead and Inveraray. In 1980 we could find no small fishing craft working on the upper loch and Auchindrain Museum's skiff had fallen to pieces. At Tighnabrugich a school had been sailing a beach skiff, but she too had been abandoned.

There were many places where a few small boats worked off open beaches all along the Highland coast and out in amongst the Western Isles. In this rugged climate, wooden craft do not last for long, but the Gairloch Heritage Museum have saved one local craft, the 31ft *Queen Mary*. She was built by MacDonald at Alligin in 1910 out of larch and elm which had been floated across Loch Torriden. The *Queen Mary* was used from 1911–1948 for great lining (long lining) for white fish and cod off Loch Torriden and occasionally she joined the herring fleet working to Stornaway in the Western Islands and even followed the herring south to the Clyde.

Out in the Western Isles a particularly seaworthy sailing beach boat was used from the west and east of the Isle of Lewis. These were the Ness sgoths, their name having originated from the protected beach of Ness, Lewis' second largest fishing centre, and sgoth is a Gaelic word for skiff. The sgoths were some of the largest open beach boats in the British Isles as they were up to 32ft long. Their hull construction with garboard fixed to a rabbetless keel was Scandinavian in origin. By the time they reached their peak of development in the 1880s the sgoths had adopted the raking stern of the Moray Firth zulu. The sgoths went, like the Shetland sixerns, up to twenty miles out into the open Atlantic. While the longlines were being set they were rowed with up to six oars, but the single dipping lug was the main source of power. Ballast of sand and shingle was carried in bags and this was dumped into the sea just before beaching.

Once the Port of Ness had about thirty-five sgoths and the last large one to go to sea was the *Peaceful* in 1947. The smaller *Jubilee*, built in 1935 was working under sail until 1947. In 1980 the Ness Historical Society restored and sailed the *Jubilee* again. The leader of this restoration was John M. Macleod, whose grandfather built the *Peaceful* in 1913 and father built *Jubilee* and he carried on the family tradition by building the *Oigh Niseach* in 1980 which was sailed 200 miles to Invergarry.

Many landings in the Highlands and Islands of western Scotland had small stone piers built during the nineteenth century. Here a net is being sorted out on the line skiff *Dawn* under the shelter of the pier at Kilchattan, Bute in 1923. The Loch Fyne skiff *Deer II* is in the background   (Dan McDonald)

Research into the fisheries of south western Scotland has been undertaken by Angus Martin and published in *Northern Studies*. In the nineteenth century there was regular contact between the Gaelic-speaking people of the Inner Hebrides, particularly Islay, and county Antrim in Northern Ireland. The Irish actually moved across to settle in the Western Isles where they usually altered their surnames to the Highland equivalent. For instance the Irish Mullens became the MacMillans and these Gaelic-speaking people did not attach much importance to which side of the North Channel they came from, but they almost always remained members of the Roman Catholic church.

Fishermen throughout the Western Islands were, in the latter half of the nineteenth century, buying secondhand luggers (scaffies, fifies and zulus) from the east coast and started working the rich, largely unnoticed fishing grounds on the west coast. The adjoining villages of Portnahaven and Portwemyss on two coves on the top of the Rinns peninsula of the Isle of Islay had by 1886 eleven 'first class' herring luggers. They also landed cod and saithe during June and July. In 1897 a vast shoal of saithe appeared and the Rinns fishermen landed 890 tons, all with hand lines. Most of this was dried and sold at the Ballycastle Lammas Fair in Northern Ireland. The forty mile passage across the open Atlantic to Ballycastle was sometimes sailed in four hours. Some years as many as 450 people crossed from Rinns and there were no language or religious barriers

28

between Antrim and Islay because they were all Gaelic-speaking Roman Catholics. Of course the Islay men were made more popular because they bought goods at Lammas Fair and many a ceilidh was held for them.

This close link explains why the 'Greencastle skiff' built in Northern Ireland, was widely used in the largely tree-less Argyll. The skiffs for the Kintyre peninsula came across on the Londonderry-Clyde steamer which stopped in the Sound of Sanda and the people of Southend rowed out and collected them. The last skiff to come across from Ireland was one from Scalasaig on Colonsay in 1926. The social link was fading away by this time although Gaelic-speaking folk were still going across on the steam-ferries to Antrim instead of crossing in fishing skiff. However, the McKays were still sailing across early in this century to visit friends and relations at their native Red Bay on the Antrim coast. The last crossing seems to have been in August 1914 when John McKay's *Little Flower* took a party of sixteen Catholics across for the dedication of a new chapel at Cushendun on the Antrim coast.

The rise of the Islay fishery had been due to huge shoals of herring on which cod and saithe fed. The Islay men used drift nets, but blamed the falling catches on the arrival of men from Campbeltown on Kintyre, who used ring-nets. This resulted in bitter feeling which reached open fighting. On one occasion in 1891 the Islay men stoned the Campbeltown skiffs so that only one could get their nets down.

In 1894 the Islay herring fishery failed and this was followed by the collapse of the line fishery for cod. The Islay men then sailed about thirty miles in June and July across the open Atlantic to the Mull of Kintyre. Here at Glemanuilt they established a fishing station. It seems that at some earlier stage of the fishery men had simply hauled the boats ashore every night and lived under the sail, but in the final years they had stone huts and slept on bracken. The tide runs very hard around Kintyre so the boats, usually about six, only went out fishing for about thirty minutes during slack water. They used baited hand lines to take cod and stainlock (mature saithe) which was dried and cured ashore.

The Mull fishery was finally halted in 1915, due to World War I, when no lights were allowed on the beach. However in the previous year only the Rinns skiffs *Lizetta*, 25ft and the 22ft *Kate*, both Irish built, had come to the Mull. Archibald Cameron's *Kate* had a meticulously varnished hull and was admired for her sailing qualities. The Islay men had a dipping lug in their skiffs, but Southend skiffs had two gaff sails. The Southend men went trapping rabbits in the winter, and in the spring they turned to creel fishing for lobsters.

The Southend fishermen joined the Islay men fishing off the Mull. The man who remembers this fishery is Hugh McShannon, born in 1901, who as a boy remembers that such vast shoals of herring passed round the Mull that the lighthouse keepers went out on the rocks at slack water and hauled them out with a bucket on a rope. Also the gannets feeding on the herring were so thick that they 'blotted out the sun.'

The Kintyre folk were mainly English-speaking Protestant Lowlanders, but they had strong Irish connections. The art of long lining was taught to Campbeltown fishermen by merchants from Portrush in Northern Ireland in the 1780s. Even in 1902 most of Campbeltown's thirty-six skiffs had been built in Portrush, county Antrim. At this time the people from Argyll and Antrim were so intermarried that they regarded themselves as one people. This link is now completely broken, and Ulster and Scotland have individual identities.

The last of the big herring luggers had been sold by 1909 but in 1980 there were still boats kept at Portnahaven and Portwemyss. On West Kintyre some six boats were kept at Machrihanish for potting in 1982. A railway from an old colliery was used to get the boats out of the water. Fishermen at beach landings all over Britain have devised different ways of getting boats ashore. The greatest drawback to working any boat off a beach is the weather, which is particularly true on the wild west coast of Scotland.

The seaworthy Greencastle skiffs which were used on both sides of the North Channel were of Scandinavian origin. In fact they had the same origin as the Shetland model, because in the late eighteenth century and early nineteenth century the ships bringing timber from Norway to Ireland also brought boats. These were known as 'Norway yawls' but when builders in Northern Ireland started to build their own versions they were called 'Druntheim' which was a local twist on the Norwegian port Trondheim from where many timber cargoes and boats were imported.

Greencastle is on the western side of Lough Foyle in county Donegal, and from the tiny beach at Ferry Point skiffs ran a passenger service across to Magilligan on the county Londonderry shore. The Druntheims here were used for lobster and handline fishing, but quite why they were sometimes known as Greencastle skiffs, no one is certain. They were not built there, but at Moville or Portrush in county Antrim. Perhaps it was because people got used to seeing them at Greencastle ferry that they associated them with the place.

The Portrush builders developed the 'Norway yawls' rather differently to those in Shetland. The Druntheims or Greencastles were long and lean with little sheer, and the sail plan was totally different to the Shetland boats. In Ireland two short masts setting spritsail or gaff sails were used. In 1900 the Congested District Board of Ireland built Druntheims for poor fishermen of Mayo and Galway. In this way the northern European tradition of shipbuilding, centred on Norway, spread round Britain and on to Ireland.

The Druntheims were up to 25ft long and some of this size were hauled up on the stony beach at Brenta Harbour near the Giant's Causeway, county Antrim, in the 1920s. The boats hauled out under the shelter of the quay at Ballycastle were also double-enders, but even before World War I transom boats were used here. The clinker transom boat, because it is more suited for fitting an engine, gradually became the indigenous boat of north west Ireland. In 1971 the *Eileen* and other double ended boats hauled out at Dunseverick, county Antrim, clearly showed the Norwegian ancestry, but the true Druntheims were virtually gone.

Michael McCaughan of the Ulster Folk & Transport Museum has recorded that in 1981 there were only five Druntheims left on the east of the Inishowen peninsula and three of those were derelict. In 1979 the Ulster Folk & Transport Museum completed the restoration of the 34ft clinker 'yawl' *Carpathia*, built at Groomsport, county Down in 1914. Groomsport and Donaghadee had been fitting auxiliary engines in their yawls since 1908, but *Carpathia* was the first one locally built with an engine. This era of motor-sail boats did not last much more than a decade, and during this period sail became unnecessary as engines improved. The *Carpathia*'s original engine was only a 7/8

30

hp petrol-paraffin single cylinder Kelvin, so for winter fishing a large dipping lug sail was set on passage and a small standing lug was kept set while handling the longlines.

The Industrial Revolution completely changed the fishing industry because it created a vast demand for protein food in the new centres of population. The wealth created by this demand, particularly with herring fishing, stimulated the building of harbours and larger boats. On the Ulster coast of county Down the new harbours of Portavogie, Ardglass and Kilkeel adopted nobbies developed from those bought from the Isle of Man, but at Ballyhalbert and many beaches to the south, open boats continued to be used off the beach. It was the practice in the area south of county Down to add the word 'port' or 'harbour' to a landing beach, such as Port Alibar, William's Harbour and Samuel's Port. Even at Newcastle (and in Antrim at Portrush) the beach was used inspite of there being a harbour. South of Newcastle to Ballymartin the Mountains of Mourne sweep down to the sea and the landings here were where the streams made natural openings in the coast.

The 21ft zulu skiff *Caliph* was built at Fraserburgh in about 1905 and later fished from Lerwick. She is seen here after being restored for pleasure sailing. Many versions of the double ended hull with dipping lug sails were used in the late nineteenth century from harbours and beaches in Scotland   (Author)

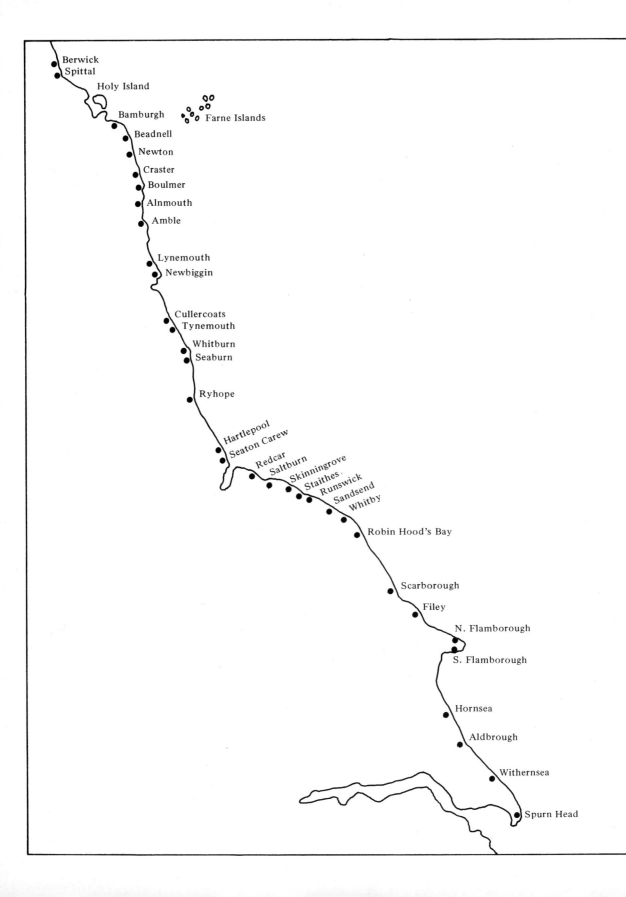

Chapter 3
The Coble Coast

The coble of the north east of England is an ancient and fascinating craft. The Celtic word for a boat is a ceubal, which seems to have progressed into coracle or currach. But there is no definite evidence as to whether the English coble did derive its name and origin from the skinboat. In 950 Alfred, a Northumbrian monk, used the word 'cuople' for a boat when writing an early English version of the Lindisfarne Gospels. Alfred might have used the word 'cuople' to mean any boat; on the other hand, he may have had a special type of boat in mind. There is no clear picture of the origin of the coble as we know it, though in a letter written in 1540 by Sir Thomas Chaloner of Guisborough it is probable that he was referring to a special type of craft similar to the boat type we know. The word coble has two different pronunciations. It is a 'cuobel' in Northumbria but becomes a 'cobble' in old Yorkshire from around the Tees to the Humber.

The feature of the 170 miles of coast between Spurn Head and the River Tweed is a total lack of natural harbours. Since the industrial revolution, several river mouths have been dredged out and new harbours created. These facilities did not exist in the Norse and medieval times, and they had to have a boat which could be landed safely on to exposed beaches in the worst weather.

The unique characteristic of the coble is that it can be beached stern first. To achieve this the hull has a deep 'grip' (forefoot) under the bow. The underwater shape curves dramatically so that the bottom under the stern is virtually flat. When coming ashore towards the beach the forefoot grips the water and the stern swings inshore, while the high pointed bow remains facing the oncoming waves. As men in the coble steady her in with flat oars (fixed on single throles) the shallow draft stern allows the coble to be washed right up to the water's edge before grounding.

The coble is basically a beach boat, but its comfortable sea-keeping qualities has meant that the hull shape has remained popular for harbour craft. The deep forefoot has forced the coble to sacrifice any pretence of speed. This forefoot made the coble difficult to sail because when pressed hard in a sudden squall the deep bow virtually tripped the coble up and caused them to 'broach' (roll over) and sink. The forefoot was also a problem when the coble was rowed. Two men rowed on the starboard side and a third man had to pull an oar over the port quarter to keep the coble going straight and counterbalance the grip of the forefoot.

Before the invention of the internal combustion engine, the craft's ability to be rowed at sea was almost more important than its sailing qualities. In really bad conditions men preferred to row, which was hard, but safer than sailing. Most of the lifeboat rescues were done under oar, and in 1838 when the steam passenger ship *Forfarshire* was driven ashore in a gale on the Farne Islands, the Longstone lighthouse keeper William Darling decided to row his coble out in a rescue attempt. The only other person available for rowing was his daughter Grace Darling. In going with her father on the first two trips to the wreck she caught the public's imagination, and she became a national hero. Anything connected with Grace Darling has been collected in a small museum at Bamburgh. The exhibition is centred on the coble that is said to have been used in the 1838 rescue. This coble is 23ft long overall and was built at Berwick-upon-Tweed in 1828 by Little Jones. It is the oldest surviving coble and has one important difference from those built later in the nineteenth century. The top plank of the side is straight up, like traditional boats, not, as in the case of a true coble, turned in to form a curved 'tumblehome' side.

The Maritime Trust have managed to save another coble, the *Blossom*, which was built much later, at Berwick-upon-Tweed, in 1887; this boat was working from Seahouses until 1969. The *Blossom* was built for a Burnmouth man but cobles were only used occasionally on the southern coast of Scotland; their normal limit was Northumbria. The *Blossom* is not a true coble because she has a pointed stern. This type is known as a round stern, or sometimes in the larger craft as a mule, the term mule coming from the cross breed between a coble and a whaling boat. The mule has less 'grip' forward than a coble.

The Hartlepool Maritime Museum have models of pointed stern cobles which were built in about 1900. These fast sailing cobles with pointed sterns were used by the Hartlepool pilots who used to go as far south as Whitby seeking incoming ships. The pointed stern cobles were chiefly used in harbour because those with square sterns tended to get knocked about when moored in lines.

Most of the sailing cobles had the square stern with sloping transom. They varied in size from about 20–40ft overall. In fact the builders turned out any size of coble the fishermen and pilots required. Most people measure a boat's length on the overall hull length but a coble's length is measured by the length of the ram plank. The ram is the length from between the bottom of the transom and approximate point where the curve of the bow starts. The overall length in a coble is usually about a third more than the ram and often more. The coble's rudder is usually a third of the overall length. In old sailing cobles the rudder had the same effect as a centreboard, and this was always unshipped and taken inboard just before beaching. When beaching, a sailing coble came in stern first controlled by two oars. The oars were flat and rested on a single pin.

The sail and oar cobles were generally narrower than the modern motor coble, and the sailing cobles had lower sides. Only about half a dozen of these sailing cobles survive and nearly all are in museums. Those that do remain are the smaller cobles used for foying (passenger and general runabouts) and for summer salmon fishing.

The only original coble sailing in the early 1980s was the 30ft overall *Sweet Promise* which was built in 1906 at Hartlepool by William Cambridge who was noted as a particularly good builder. The *Sweet Promise* has been totally rebuilt by Hector

Handyside of Amble, a particular labour of love for him because Hector's grandfather was a coble fisherman at Beadnell and he is the master builder at Harrison's Yard, Amble.

In the early years of this century coble building seems to have declined in Northumbria and fishermen ordered their new boats from builders in Hartlepool and Filey which were delivered by rail. Harrison's yard did not start to concentrate on cobles until about 1912, but they have been building according to demand ever since. This yard, beside the tiny River Coquet at Amble, is the only building centre north of the Tees.

The centre of coble building is Whitby. The skills of wooden boat construction was kept alive in North Yorkshire by the Whitby Boat Building Company and the men who trained in this yard started their own enterprises. In recent years the coble builders at Whitby have been William Clarkson, Gordon Clarkson and J. N. Lowther; just north of the town at Sandsend C. A. Goodall has a yard. 'Tony' Goodall's father had been the station master so that when the railway closed he was able to buy the station. The old railway shed became the shop for building small boats and larger cobles were built outside. Between 1951–82 Goodall, with the help of one or two men, had built 165 boats, mostly large motor cobles.

The first engines were fitted in cobles before World War I, but this was only in those working from harbours. The great problem was that right aft, where the propeller needed to be, the coble was flat bottomed. This made it very difficult to beach a coble fitted with the motor because it was so easy to damage the propeller and drive shaft. At least three different solutions have been found to this problem: by a tunnel under the stern in which the three bladed propeller turns, by raising the ram plank aft so that the propeller revolved higher than the bottom, or having a universal coupling in the prop shaft so that the two bladed propeller can be hoisted up out of harms way for beaching. The early petrol engines were fairly low powered, so that most cobles retained sails, but these were used less and less so that when fishermen ordered new boats they no longer required the sailing hulls. Motor cobles have the same basic hull shape, but they are much fuller in the bow and generally more beamy, with higher sides and less draught. Even in the days of sail the big 'herring cobles' from Filey had a foredeck which formed a cuddy where some of the crew could shelter from the worst weather. When motors became general, all new Yorkshire cobles were given foredecks and then wheelhouses as well. North of the Tees in the early 1980s, most cobles remained open like the old sailing 'winter cobles', but with a hood carried over the bows. When motoring into a headsea this saves the coble and its crew from being swamped by spray. If the hood creates too much windage while picking up fleets of pots, the hood can be dropped, while a wheelhouse would remain a permanent fixture.

As well as wooden motor cobles, another type, the double-ended surf boat is preferred by some beach fishermen, particularly at Withernsea, Filey and Runswick. When talking to builders and fishermen on the coast, they all agreed that the double-ended coble is not a recent invention. The fact that it is most common south of the Tees suggests that it is either a descendant of the Victorian mule, although they were only popular for a few years, or that it is a result of Norfolk fishermen moving up to this area with their crab boats. The double-ender is a very different craft from the coble, although both are wooden and clinker-built. In many ways the double-ender is easier to beach, as it can come in bows first and keep the rudder in place.

A change in the type of salmon net used has resulted in the salmon coble vanishing from beaches of the north-east of England and being replaced by the surf boat. The salmon and sea trout swim near the surface and are taken with a drift net under licence. These nets were very bulky when made of cotton; the man-made material nets are much lighter and only require a small boat. There were different ways of salmon fishing, but just to show how much net was involved, a Northumbrian fleet of six nets was 600 yards in length.

The salmon coble was a small version of the winter coble, but it was still a heavy craft to move about on the beach. When the man-made salmon nets were introduced, they took up less space and were much lighter so that it was more practical to use the double-ended clinker surf boats which floated in a few inches of water. When tending the nets, these could be rowed in either direction which saved the bother of turning them round. The flat oars on a single throle pin are still used. They can be left while tending the nets and will not fall in the water. The cotton nets were thick and could be seen by the fish so they always had to be used after dark, while the thin transparent man-made net can be used in daylight. To conserve stocks, salmon fishing is licenced, and today only poachers fish at night off the coast.

The River Tweed is the main salmon fishing area and the water bailiff has to catch the poachers with salmon actually in their possession. Poaching sometimes takes place here in broad daylight and the man only has to let go of the net or discard the fish to be free of prosecution. As the Tweed is the most prolific salmon river in the country, it has been divided into separate fisheries since medieval times. The boats used are flat-bottomed, so they go in shallow water and have a wide stern over which the nets are paid out. The Lees of Spittal who built these boats called them punts although they are also known as cobles. The larger 22ft version, the sea coble, was used along the coast near the Tweed mouth. In 1974 I saw a whole string of these Tweed salmon cobles lying at Spittal, but in 1980 they were being replaced by ordinary GRP boats. Outside the Tweed a salmon coble was the term used for a traditional coble. This type has been kept alive not in wood, but in plastic.

In 1965 Colin Wigglesworth of Scarborough took the shape of a 17ft coble built by the renowned Flamborough builder 'Arg' Hopwood and produced the first glass-reinforced plastic coble. These were sold as the Yorkshire Coble class and in 1967 another series was started with the shape of a 24ft 6in Hopwood coble. These longer cobles proved to be much better sailers than the 17 footers. Most of these GRP cobles are powered by outboards in a trunk in the stern, a system which works well because the GRP cobles are mainly used by part-time fishermen and anglers who can store their outboards at home. Colin Wigglesworth believes that he has produced about seven hundred GRP Yorkshire Cobles in seventeen years.

The reason for keeping to the traditional hull shape, which after all had taken many hundreds of years to evolve, was because they are good for beaching. One 17ft Yorkshire Coble came ashore through what were believed to be 15ft waves at Saltburn. The two men in the coble were thrown helplessly into the bottom and the sky went black as the wave curled above them, yet the coble survived the breaking water and was

36

A salmon coble at Spittal in about 1925. At Berwick and on the east coast of Scotland the salmon coble was a flat bottomed boat for working in shallow water   (Rev H. S. Ross)

washed safely up the beach. Any boat is only as good as the men in it. I once watched some beginners trying to launch a new 17ft GRP coble off the South Landing, Flamborough. The man rowing did not react quickly enough and the coble was flung sideways on the beach, trapping one of the launchers underneath. He was lucky to get away with a soaking.

The places where the cobles land regularly are spread along some 170 miles of coast. Every landing is totally different and the presence of the boats and fishing communities give them strong individual identities. At the northern end, there are the lonely sandy beaches of Northumbria. Bamburgh is dominated by the huge castle overlooking the sea. At one time boats carried tourists on trips from the beach here.

North Sunderland used to be the main fishing centre for this part of the coast until the harbour was built at Seahouses in 1889, when the latter replaced it. The village of Beadnell also has a harbour, which was originally used by trading vessels coming to the lime kiln. The fishermen worked off two different beaches at Beadnell; indeed the huts and pots are still stored on the cliff top, but about three cobles now operate out of the tiny harbour. Across Beadnell Bay is Newton by the Sea which, in living memory, had seven cobles; but in 1982 only one remained.

Boulmer has a community virtually dependent on boats fishing off an open beach. In the early nineteenth century there were hundreds of such places round the coast of Britain, but since then the whole economic and social world has changed. The population of Britain has multiplied at an astonishing rate. The tide of people borne, first by the railways and then by cars, swept out to fill every corner of Britain. The lonely isolated fishing communities of the past have been swamped by tourists and a new residential population. Boulmer is one of the only remaining places where the bulk of the community depend on beach-based fishing.

The cobles at Boulmer are kept on moorings in The Haven most of the time. This is a pool off the sandy beach which is protected by off-lying rocky reefs. There is always enough water in the main entrance to enter the haven, but in really bad weather this haven does not live up to its name. A southerly wind makes Boulmer Haven particularly exposed. If the wind rises suddenly the fishermen often get up in the night and get their cobles 'on the wheels' and up on to the beach. Even then cobles are occasionally swamped and sunk.

In the nineteenth century Boulmer was the local centre of the herring fishing because of the railway just a mile away at Longhoughton which was the nearest point to the Northumbrian coast. At that period there were two curing houses at Boulmer and 'Bart' Stanton used to say that he could remember seeing fifty-two herring boats at once in the Haven. This changed when a harbour was built at Craster in 1904–05 to ship stone away from the quarry. Craster at that stage had over twenty cobles, and when the harbour was built it turned into a herring centre. The quarry closed in 1939 and Seahouses became the fish landing centre, but Craster still had four boats and the smoke houses still remained in use for kippering herring.

In evidence given to the Inspector of Fisheries in 1878, George Stevenson said that Boulmer had ten long line boats and fourteen boats for the herring season. Stevenson said that in his lifetime – he was talking of the mid-Victorian period – the number of line boats (cobles) on the coast had risen. The price of fish had risen, but the catches had got smaller. The inshore fishermen of the North East were complaining bitterly at that time that the new steam trawlers were destroying the feeding grounds and ruining the fish stocks. The cry was much the same all round the coast, but there also seems to have been a rapid rise in the number of inshore boats as well as steam vessels based in industrial fishing ports between 1880–1910. The result was undoubtedly over-fishing and literally thousands of inshore fishermen working off beaches had to seek other employment.

Boulmer's fishing community survived the two decades of economic depression between the wars. In the early 1920s there were fifteen cobles here, while in 1982 there were eight. This sounds like a decline, but as George Stanton explained, the motor cobles are much larger than the old sailing cobles. Some of the local cobles are 42ft overall, although George's own *Margaretta* is only 28ft overall (this fact had to be looked up, as like a true cobleman, he only knew the ram length – 19ft in this case). The first capstan for hauling pots was fitted in 1948, but George Stanton remembers his family's coble *Primrose* being fitted with an engine in about 1927 and in the following few years all the Boulmer cobles followed suit. The older fishermen, however, hated those engines and would stop them at the slightest excuse. The engine was stopped if there was a lightest chance of a sailing breeze and in a calm the boys were often made to row home, a source of some dispute between generations!

Working the sailing cobles called for a total commitment by the whole community. The women had to get up with the men in the early hours of the morning as it was their job to fill the ballast sacks while the cobles were taken down to either of the Haven's two entrances. Just before daylight (often this was 4.30 a.m.) when the cobles went to sea, the women returned home and 'skinned' mussels and baited 600 hooks. This was half a longline, and when the men returned at about 11 a.m. they baited the other half. Each of the three men in a coble's crew brought a longline so that each coble was setting 3600 baited hooks.

In the 'Fishing Boat' Inn at Boulmer, (which stands in the middle of the line of neat grey stone cottages which follow the road as it runs near the coast) is a splendid romantic Victorian painting showing the women dragging the lifeboat into the water. This was a true scene and this custom took place at most beach landings. The women helped with the hard work ashore so that the men would go to sea fresh. The lifeboat needed hours of heavy rowing to reach her rescue and the men needed all their strength to keep it up and return safely. It might seem that women in the pre-engine fishing villages were oppressed. It is true that they never stopped working – they often knitted as they walked – but oppressed is doubtful. The women were a vital part of the fishing community and were so closely involved in it that it helped to bind the whole community into almost one large family, which, because of intermarriage, they almost were.

The introduction of the motor coble and the abandoning of longlines has released the women from their unpaid role in the longshore fishing here. At Boulmer a real sense of community remains, as the coble men live in the village. They started their own lifeboat society when the RNLI withdrew its boat in 1969. The village is attractive without being beautiful. The really beautiful villages along the coast attract tourism, and this, with all its amusement junk, drives the fishermen back into the housing estates and weakens the sense of community. The other great killer of a fishing community is the 'holiday home' village, but since Boulmer is part of the estate of the Duke of Northumberland, that threat is kept away. The Duke claims the salmon rights for 1,000 yards from the low water mark, but anyone living in his cottages has the right to fish free.

It is not only the Duke who seeks to control the taking of salmon. The Northumbrian Water Authority licences only 127 people in the county to fish for salmon. Today salmon and indeed the lobster and crab landed at Boulmer are sent to faraway Grimsby by a fishermen's cooperative shared with Holy Island. Even before World War II all the crab and lobster were sent to the 'barrow boys' in the industrial towns of the Midlands.

The extinction of longlining off the Northumbrian coast is blamed on the trawlers who steamed through the lines. In some cases such as at Alnmouth the fishing communities died out when longlining was abandoned. In 1973 Jack Stewart, then eighty-two years old and the last remaining Alnmouth fisherman, recalled that the main problem with longlining was getting the bait. In his father's time the fishermen had to pay the crews of the Amble collier brigs to bring back bait from Holland or southern England. In around 1910, when there were eight mule cobles working from Alnmouth, the bait, which was mussels, came from Morecambe Bay or King's Lynn by rail, an instance of one form of longshore fishing supporting another.

Up to the headland at Lynmouth, the coast is flanked by rural farmland and south of it is industrial; coal mining is in evidence right down to the Tees. Near Lynmouth beach is a huge gypsy encampment, complete with lorries, caravans and ponies and even canvas-topped waggons. The gypsies are working the coal from the tips of Lynmouth Colliery. Sea-coal gathering by old, young and unemployed is a common sight on the beaches from Lynmouth to Seaton Carew. At Dene Mouth the local collieries produce enough waste to support a little coal industry of full-time beach-coalers. The colliery town of Ashington joins up and almost swamps the beach fishing village of Newbiggin. In 1831, long before coal mining led to the industrialisation of the coast, Newbiggin was a hamlet with eight cobles. By 1878 Newbiggin had twenty-seven cobles. These were built in the village, and had the reputation for being particularly seaworthy. The fine bow Northumbrian cobles were launched into a breaking sea which would have overwhelmed an ordinary boat.

Newbiggin still had twenty cobles in 1939, which were engaged in herring drifting in the summer and long lining in the winter. Like Boulmer cobles, their territory was about ten miles either side of the landing and four miles to seaward. In 1982 eight cobles were working from Newbiggin full time, while three more joined in for the summer salmon fishing. The cobles used to be kept on the sand in front of the church, but this is now left to pleasure boats and the old lifeboat slide is used as a landing. In recent decades erosion has been a considerable problem at Newbiggin. The headland with the church on it is protected by rock, but the sand in front of the rows of terraced houses has no resistance to the wave action. A row of concrete blocks, placed in World War II on the beach in front to prevent tanks landing, have long since fallen into the sea. In 1982 a new concrete breakwater was completed out from the church headland to break the force of the waves driving into the concrete slope in front of the houses. This breakwater was greatly cursed by the coble men because they considered it inadequate.

Continuing south, the next beach landing is Cullercoats, just north of the entrance of the River Tyne. Before the present Tyne entrance was blasted out of rock and dredged deeper, Cullercoats, on the open coast, was an ideal place to work a fishing boat. There was also a ready-made market for fish in the city of Newcastle-upon-Tyne. In 1815, there were ten cobles working from the sheltered cove in front of the cliff-top village of Cullercoats. By 1878 there were forty-three winter cobles supporting about eight hundred people here. This rose to at least sixty cobles which filled both sides of the beach, and they were stored on the roads leading to beaches and on 'Boat Hill' on the southern cliff top.

In the days of sail, Cullercoats had the largest number of boats for a beach landing in the north east of England. Only a few men were full-time fishermen; many spent part of the year working in shipyards on the Tyne. While shipbuilding and mining boomed in the towns lining the Tyne, people wanted a place to relax and Whitley Bay, with its golden beach was developed as a coastal resort. The old fishing village of Cullercoats was virtually flattened and the coastal strip was covered with rows of neat Edwardian brick villas. However, the fishermen did manage to get a breakwater built to protect the beach.

In 1982 there were five cobles working from Cullercoats and some more part-timers

The cobles at Cullercoats in 1982 including the long narrow Northumbrian coble *James Denyer* in the centre and the Whitby built *Argonaut*, with a foredeck and wheelhouse, on back left   (Author)

kept their cobles and mules up beside the cliff road. These cobles only go about one and half miles offshore 'until the piers open' (that is the piers on either side of the Tyne mouth) then they are on the 'soil', an area of clay bottom with a few rocky patches, which they work. The seasons are salmon from May to August and then potting until October. In the old days this was the start of the longlining season, but since the introduction of man-made thread, monofilate cod nets are used. These are anchored to the bottom between buoys.

After Cullercoats, the next place where boats are still landed is Whitburn, but there are now only about fifty assorted pleasure boats here. The beach at Whitburn is typical of most of the north east. The top end is flat and sandy while at low tide there is a mass of flat rocks. The bay between Whitburn and Seaburn, where there is no trace of the old coble landing, is now a resort for nearby Sunderland. South of the River Wear is the village of Ryhope which is reputed to have been a coble landing. However, erosion is eating away the soft clay cliffs, so that the road ends abruptly and there is nowhere to store a boat.

In the days of sail Hartlepool had a coble fleet working off the Fish Sands, a now empty beach on the landward side of the Heugh headland. South of Seaham the word coble is pronounced 'cobble', but the type built in the days of sail was the long lean 'Northumbrian' coble with a cut away grip (forefoot) to allow for easier beaching. The Hartlepool builders, Cambridge, had a reputation for producing the best sailing cobles.

Longlining appears to have been a very ancient practice at Hartlepool, as iron hooks dating from the fourteenth century have been excavated in Lumley Street. The Hodgson family were for many decades fish hook makers in the town. Later, fish curing houses were built on the Croft and the Fish Sands were protected by a stone pier.

The Hartlepool Maritime Museum have the interior of a cottage in Fisher Row, a row of eighteenth century cottages, on display. Because of the lack of space on the Heugh these cottages were very cramped, but it was generally poverty that forced two families to share one cottage. The single room was a kitchen and living room, with a bed as a kind of bunk under the stairs with a curtain across. Since the fishermen often worked at night and slept during the day, curtains were used to create darkness. In other parts of the country fishermen had four-poster beds so that they could have darkness to sleep during the day. At Hartlepool the 'line houses' where the women baited the longlines, were at the back of the cottages. Mussels gathered locally were used as bait and the children were also sent to catch shrimp for bait.

To allow better access to the busy Fish Sands where the boats landed and the catch was auctioned, the Sandwell Gate in the walled town was widened but in 1880 a fish quay was erected in the docks. By this time coal exporting was booming and the docks of new West Hartlepool filled in the bay behind the Heugh. In 1910 the fish-landing quay was built in the Victoria Dock and although Hartlepool still has cobles in its fishing fleet, the beach landing has long since been abandoned.

The same is true of Seaton Carew, which is at the southern end of Hartlepool Bay. The sandy beach at Seaton has made it a popular resort, but its position just at the entrance of the Tees means that pilots used to work from here, in cobles painted black to distinguish them from fishing cobles. The Lithgo family of Seaton Carew held Tees Pilot Licences continuously from 1760 until well into this century.

The Tees pilots also worked from Redcar on the southern side of the Tees and sometimes used a double-ended coble. These had to be fast as the pilots raced to reach incoming ships first; also, if they picked up a ship down the coast, the coble was towed stern first. There is a lot of surf in the shallow water off Redcar and the pointed stern was good for these conditions. These boats were also better for 'foying' (running pleasure trips) in the summer.

The pilot cobles at Redcar were sailed two handed, by a pilot and his crew or 'dog'. When the pilot boarded a ship the 'dog' sailed the coble home. One of the dodges to get ahead of his rivals used by pilot 'Darkie' Guy of the coble *Try Again* was to pay a man in Filey to telegraph him when a ship was coming up the coast so that he could go down and meet it first. During World War I the Redcar pilots had to work from the examination boat off the Tees mouth and they never returned to using beach cobles.

Redcar and the adjoining Coatham were described as 'fashionable bathing resorts' in 1817 and the flat beach of golden sands still attracts visitors. For a boat to reach this beach it has to come in through the scars, a mass of rocks. The main channel is in the Lay with another channel into it on the north side called the Luff Way. To aid the coble men in, there are guiding marks in the town which they line up to keep in the all important channel. Even the fishermen have to wait for the right conditions before leaving the beach. After a gale it can take several days for the swell to settle down.

In the early 1970s only about six cobles remained working from Redcar; since then, as in so many places, state aid has helped to increase the number of inshore boats. In the past the fishermen had to finance their own boats. This often called for personal hardship such as an incident in 1862 when the Redcar fisherman Picknett ordered a new coble from Cambridge of Hartlepool. For three weeks before the new coble arrived the weather was so bad that Picknett could not go off and earn any money, yet he would not allow his family to touch the money set aside for the new coble. Instead they had to live off salted herring and potatoes.

Since World War II the White Fish Authority loans have helped to finance the purchase of boats and gear by a number of part-time fishermen so that they can work full-time. These loans have led to a steady increase in the Redcar fleet so that by 1982 twenty-one cobles were working off the beach. Typical of the new generation of motor coble is the *Silver Jubilee*, built in 1977 for E. Smith and I. Muirhead. She is fitted with a 72 hp diesel engine, hydraulic capstan, VHF radio and echo sounder. The *Silver Jubilee* was originally open forward with a hood, but in 1982, like the larger cobles *Audrey Lass*, *Freedom* and *Jane Marie*, she was decked forward with a wheelhouse. Only a few Redcar working cobles such as the *Whimbrel* still had a hood.

In the summer the Redcar cobles work up to six miles offshore for salmon. They also lay fleets of pots until October and then use gill nets anchored to the bottom. In the winter, when the cobles return in the late morning, they line up on the beach and retail haddock, plaice and cod over the side of their boats to the public. After this the boats

The coble *Silver Jubilee* lined up with other Redcar cobles for retailing fresh fish on the beach, 1982 (Author)

are towed on their trailers by tractors up the sea road to their places on the Esplanade. No one locally takes the slightest notice of the large cobles going through the traffic on the sea front, nor at them stopping at the filling station to fill up with diesel.

East of Redcar the coast starts to change as the low ground gives way to cliffs. This is Cleveland, an old name meaning 'cliff land'. The impressive cliffs are at the seaward edge of the Cleveland hills and the North York Moors.

At Saltburn the cliff is only just starting to rise and there is a wide stony beach near the beck mouth used by fifty boats. None of these are worked full time, and although most are surf boats, there are a wide variety of craft including GRP cobles and even a Norfolk crab boat. The beaches of Britain are a splendid place to find veteran tractors. Saltburn's numerous tractors are virtually an agricultural museum. There are not only the customary 1960s Ford Majors, but Saltburn even has 1950 TVO Fordsons.

While Redcar and Saltburn are pleasure resorts, the next landing continuing south east is Skinningrove, an industrial village in a steep valley leading down to a tiny beach protected by a pier. This stone pier was built for flat-bottomed steamers which delivered goods for the steelworks on the hill top. Most of the men work in the steelworks or at the potash works at Boulby and fish part-time. About twenty boats, mostly surf boats are kept at Skinningrove and many are owned by men living inland.

Another great interest of Skinningrove men is pigeon racing. The valley sides are dotted with fishermen's sheds and pigeon lofts. The local council had decided to clear up the beach area, but the fishermen formed themselves into an association to do this themselves, while in 1982 the council had the sheds painted a uniform green. The men seemed to look upon fishing as being a break from the better-paid but monotonous work at the steelworks, although in October 1982 about thirty men were milling about near the sheds, many of them out of work.

One of the Skinningrove men told me that seals were a problem, killing the fish and destroying the nets. One morning he had found a young seal washed up by the gale up to the road. He had carried the seal back to the sea because it was such an appealing sight with its big mournful eyes. However, when he got out to his nets he found that they had been ripped badly by a seal and he 'wished he had shot the bugger' instead of putting it back into the sea.

East of Skinningrove is Boulby Cliff, rising some 700ft from the sea, the highest perpendicular cliff in England. The cliffs have sloped down by the time Staithes (locally pronounced Steers) is reached. The grey stone houses at Staithes are packed tightly together in a steep valley, with the fast flowing Colburn beck running down the valley floor and forming a tidal inlet. Staithes grew after the fifteenth century and its prosperity was founded on fishing and ironstone mining. In 1817 the Rev. George Young wrote that there were seventy cobles working from Staithes and in 1861 one account said that the village had 120 boats. When the railway reached Staithes in 1885 it ran three special trains a week to transport fish out.

In the days of sail the fishermen of Staithes, like most fishermen of that time, were very superstitious. There was no real explanation for weather patterns or the habits of the fish, so they thought these were directed by supernatural forces. The only way to overcome this magic was to observe certain rituals. A fisherman would not go to sea if he heard the mention of a four legged animal, particularly a pig. It was extremely bad

44

luck to meet a woman wearing white linen on the way to the boats. However if the woman turned her back on the men then the force of evil was overcome and the 'bad luck' removed. When a coble had a run of poor catches the wives of the crew met at midnight and in silence they killed a pigeon, took out its heart and stuck it full of pins and burnt it over a charcoal fire.

Staithes folk were no more superstitious that any other fishing community; it is just that their customs have been recorded. In the early nineteenth century the lives of people in rural coastal Britain were still influenced by beliefs that had their origins in pagan gods and had been gradually altered over the centuries. These beliefs were frowned upon by the Christian church and were therefore kept secret. It was the nonconformists or 'chapel people' who came to rescue the eternal souls of the fishermen of Staithes. Their straightforward form of worship caught the imagination of the humble Staithes people and they built a Wesley Church, a Primitive Methodist chapel and a Bethel on the winding streets leading down to the beck. Once a week on Sunday the men, wives and children dressed up in their best clothes and went to chapel to hear stories from the Bible adapted by the forthright preachers into terms they understood.

Staithes as a major fishing centre was killed by steam trawlers and drifters working from deepwater harbours. The larger first class boats which were double-ended herring mules of about 35ft overall, and with a crew of five, were the first to go. From a peak of around sixteen in 1879 the numbers dwindled until only the *Charity* remained in 1912 and finally gave up in 1920.

The big cobles were the next to go. These were about 32ft overall and were very heavy because they were fitted with skids so that they could be dragged up the beach. Since there were no horses available, the women had to assist with the heavy manual work of hauling the cobles ashore up on to Seaton Garth beach in front of the town. At sea these cobles were fast. Like all cobles they set a dipping lug, but they were higher-peaked so that they could catch any upper wind when sailing inshore close to the high ground.

The coble was capable, in favourable conditions, of sailing fast. Once a coble taking a man to his wedding sailed the sixteen miles from Staithes to Hartlepool in 1 hour 20 minutes which works out at 12 knots.

In 1923 the *Mizpah* was the first Staithes coble to be fitted with an engine and a little later a harbour wall was built to try and save the fishing, but to no avail. By 1951 there was only one coble working full time from Staithes and five others catering for the tourist trade. Since then there has been something of a revival; true, it is still a long way from 1887 when 224 fishermen worked from here, but by 1977 there were four full-time cobles and four part-time boats fishing. In 1978 the new trammel nets anchored on the sea bed were first used and by 1982 there were about twenty boats lying in the beck. The bright colours of their paint work contrasted sharply with the grey of the houses and the cliff.

In the past the double-ended boat at Staithes was known as a jolly boat. There were not many of these as in Victorian photographs of Staithes and near-by Runswick only cobles can be seen hauled out. The beach at Runswick is firm sand while the high ground surrounding the bay makes it very sheltered. However the ground rises so steeply from the beach that storing the boats is a problem. The cobles were dragged by a hand winch up on a steep ramp beside the lifeboat shed. In 1971 a concrete wall was built to

Cobles at Staithes in about 1960   (E. Philip Dobson)

stop erosion and on top of this was created a boat park linked to the beach with a concrete slip. The hills around the bay are looked on with some dissatisfaction by the fishermen as they shelter the sea and when the wind is 'off land' the water becomes clear and the fish have more of a chance of seeing the trammel nets.

In 1982 there were twelve double-ended boats at Runswick including *Liberator* which was fully equipped with a net hauler, working lights and even ship-to-shore radio. Only one small coble was kept here and the last sailing coble, fitted with an engine, was sold away in 1952. In fact fishing virtually died out here and has restarted.

The same is true of Sandsend. The last salmon coble was sold away in 1939, but now several part-timers use surf boats for fishing off the beach. However the part-timers are greatly resented by the full-time fishermen of nearby Whitby. In the winter many of the surf boats are stored in Tony Goodall's yard at Sandsend.

The beach at Sandsend is a wide expanse of sand, but the next landing, south of Whitby is Robin Hood's Bay and is a very difficult place to come ashore. The old name for the village was Baytown but local legend said that the hero of Sherwood Forest used the village as a hideout. The houses are very nearly on the cliff edge and line a steep narrow road leading down to the rocky foreshore. A narrow channel, 'The Landing', runs from the road out to the sea. On either side are the scars (reefs) which are covered at high tide. The channel was marked with posts, but in the days of sail many cobles were lost when attempting to land here in bad weather.

46

At Robin Hood's Bay cobles were brought ashore on two-wheel carts, a common practice on Yorkshire beaches, and then dragged up the slipway to an area known as 'the dock'. In 1840 there were about thirty cobles and five-man keel boats working from here. In those days bad weather, when the boats could not go out, meant no money coming in and the families literally went hungry. The fishermen's wives had to be able to budget and always keep money aside for the weeks when fishing was poor.

In the 1930s Leo Walmsley, who was born at Robin Hood's Bay, published novels such as *Three Fevers* and *Sound of the Sea*, which gave a real insight into the days of hardship and sail. Dame Laura Knight wrote about Staithes in the days when every man, woman and child were totally committed to fishing. At Staithes the women and children had to walk up to fifteen miles down the coast to gather enough mussels for the longline bait.

Such conditions are no longer part of longshore fishing. Robin Hood's Bay is now largely a residential and holiday village protected against cliff erosion by a sea wall built in 1975. At that time there were only two boats working from this landing. One of these was used by Andrew Young, landlord of the Laurel Inn, for potting, while Tom Jenkinson had a new 26ft coble built by Clarkson at Whitby. The price of a coble has changed so much that the monetary terms are of little meaning but before 1914 a new coble was £1 a foot. In the mid-1950s this had reached £51 a foot with an engine. In the

The double ender *Liberator* about to leave Runswick in 1982 to haul trammel nets. She was fully equipped with net hauler, lights and radio   (Author)

mid-1970s it had become £184 a foot while with inflation galloping by 1982 the price was £620 per foot.

The Yorkshire coast is inhospitable until Filey. From Filey Brigg headland there are six miles of flat sandy beach protected at the south east by Flamborough Head. Filey Bay is shallow, with banks, and in a blow the seas break dangerously close inshore. The cobles working from Filey use a section of the beach tucked behind Filey Brigg. There has been commercial fishing from Filey for at least eight hundred years and the boats from here were going to the Yarmouth herring fishery long before harbours were built at Scarborough and Bridlington. Filey reached a peak in about 1870 when some four hundred fishermen lived in the town. The big herring mules were often over 40ft and were called 'sploshers' because of the noise they made in a seaway. These proved a bit mighty for beaching and were often based at Scarborough for the herring season. The Filey men also bought even larger Yorkshire yawls which sometimes discharged on Filey beach, but mostly worked from Scarborough. (Although Scarborough had a harbour it is worth mentioning that there was still some beach work. Colliers and the herring fleet used to discharge on the beach to avoid paying harbour dues. In the Edwardian period cobles also ran pleasure trips off stages on the beach).

In 1897 Canon A. N. Cooper commented that Filey had changed from being a fishing village with a few visitors' lodgings to a fashionable watering place with a few fishermen. Filey, like most seaside towns, certainly grew as a resort in the Victorian period, but unlike many, it retained its fishing fleet. In a way the visitors helped the fishermen to earn a living at a period when steam trawlers from such ports as Hull and Grimsby were flooding the market with fish. The cobles ran pleasure trips from July to September.

Filey beach has firm sand, but being flat the tide recedes a considerable distance. In *Customs of Yorkshire*, published in 1814, there is an aquatint of fishermen bringing a coble ashore on a trolley at Filey. Later in that century the heavy herring and winter cobles were taken up the beach on trolleys pulled by three horses. Horses were not always available, however, so eight 'launchers', usually retired fishermen, hauled a coble on a trolley down to the sea. Donkeys were used to bring up the nets and lines. In 1954 Don 'Cherry' Mason hit on the idea of using a tractor to tow the coble trolleys. This simple innovation saved a great deal of hard work and made 'Cherry' Mason a local hero. Since then a Tractor Society has been formed, its members bought a tractor and employed Yulbert Clubley to drive the tractor.

The cobles are stored ashore on a wide ramp and promenade known as the Coble Landing. In the 1920s the fishermen paid a nominal rent to Sir Dennis Bailey for the landing. This local landowner, as Lord of the Manor, claimed the sea for as far as a javelin could be thrown. Once a year on a very low tide a man on horseback would ride out into the sea and throw a javelin in order to maintain this ancient right. The coble landing was bought by a Scarborough trawler owner in the 1930s and then in 1971 the Filey Council purchased it.

There were sixty-four cobles at Filey in 1866, but when the first engine was fitted in 1920 the number had dropped to forty-five and was to go on declining. The last coble was built at Filey in 1947 and by 1962 only eight cobles were left working. However something of a recovery had started because by 1971 there were ten cobles working full time and a few more joined for the winter fishing. In 1974 there were sixteen cobles working and the largest was the 31ft length overall *Advance* built in 1959. Stanley 'Trabb' Cammish was working the 29ft 6in length overall *Alison & Adrian* built in 1967. Wheelhouses are not popular at Filey, although the old sailing herring cobles here were fitted with foredecks way back in the early nineteenth century.

In 1974 Filey was one of the few remaining longlining centres in Eastern England. The cobles usually worked between three and six miles off shore, but occasionally they went as far as twenty miles. Each coble laid out twelve longlines over a distance of about four miles. When the last line was shot, the coble returned to the other end and hauling was started. The great art was to lay out the longlines so as not to foul another coble's lines. For this an intricate unwritten pattern has been evolved over the years. The longlines are also laid out so that the rival Scarborough and Bridlington trawlers cannot (hopefully) get among them. On a good day a coble would hope to land about a quarter of a ton of codling with longlines.

Girls 'skaning' mussels at Whitby in about 1890 for baiting longlines   (F. M. Sutcliffe)

Handling the longlines is hard work and as one Filey fisherman put it 'If everyone in Britain worked as hard as fishermen we could call this country Great Britain'. Each coble has a crew of two or three, but a shore gang is also employed, usually another three, of openers and baiters for preparing the long lines in sheds. Since women are quicker with their hands than men, most of the mussel opening is done by them. A good opener can open six cwt of mussels in an hour. The baiters are usually retired fishermen. Between March and the autumn the Filey boats are potting for lobster and crab, while some men have salmon licences. In 1984 longlining and potting were keeping fifteen Filey cobles working all the year.

The beautiful sandy beach at Filey makes it a popular resort with holiday camps outside the town. In spite of this ever-changing influx of people, the coble landing is the centre of a thriving longshore fishing community. The Filey Fishermen's Choir now has members from other employments, but it still sings hymns with all the feeling of the Victorian Christian. The longshore fishermen are mostly clannish and kindhearted under a guarded exterior. On shore the fishermen are generous and helpful to one another, but afloat they are rivals.

South of Filey the coast sweeps boldly out to form the 400ft high Flamborough Head. Flamborough stands back from the exposed headland and except for a few GRP cobles and neat stacks of crab pots in a few gardens, it looks as if it could be an inland village.

The cobles *Imperialist* and *Prosperity* hauled up at the North Landing, Flamborough. In the days of sail, cobles were hauled out here by a steam capstan while at the South Landing horses were used   (Author)

The boats work from the North and South Landings which are coves in the chalk cliffs on either side of Flamborough Head. The South Landing, which has the level ground for dragging a boat ashore, seems to have been the one used in the past. In 1794 twenty fishermen were drowned working from the South Landing. Both landings were used in the late nineteenth century according to the weather. Northerly breezes saw the cobles coming ashore at the South Landing, where they were hauled ashore by horse, while the North Landing was used in a southerly breeze.

The North Landing at Flamborough is one of the most impressive beach landings in Britain. In a northerly wind a swell builds up in the narrow channel and in a north-easterly the sea comes straight in, turning the whole cove into a boiling mass of white water. The cobles come in between high chalk cliffs and then have to be hauled up a very steep slope. In about 1900 a steam capstan was fitted to do the hauling. This cannot have been very satisfactory because in about 1912 a Crossley horizontal single cylinder petrol paraffin engine was installed for hauling, replaced more recently by a diesel engine. The petrol-paraffin engines were widely used in boats until the late 1950s. They started on the expensive petrol and then when hot were switched over to the cheaper paraffin. To stop the engine the process had to be reversed and if the engine stalled the carburettor had to be drained of paraffin.

The slope is so steep at the North Landing that donkeys were used to carry fish and gear up to the cliff top and back to the village. Before World War I Flamborough was a remote place with its own very strong dialect and customs. The Flamborough Sword Dance is well known and another local custom was the autumn 'Raising the Herring' when women dressed up as men and went through the village singing. Such customs usually go back to pagan times, but were kept going because they brightened up the year in an age when people made all their own entertainment. Just about everyone attended the Christian church or chapel, but most fisher folk still firmly believed in superstition. They went to church to pray, but at the same time kept up the old customs just in case. People who depended on anything as temperamental as the sea could not afford to take chances. The fisher folk's lives were directed by the mood of the weather and they knew when the fish came and went, but they had absolutely no explanation as to why it all happened.

Before World War I there were about sixty cobles at the North Landing and about fifty at the South Landing. Some families kept a boat at each landing and worked them according to the weather. Most of the cobles were built in the village by the Hopwoods. The last of these was Hargreaves 'Arg' Hopwood who died in 1939. He was something of a legendary builder as he worked behind closed doors and produced beautifully shaped cobles single-handed. The only help Arg Hopwood asked for was when the coble had to be turned over so that the drafts (skids) could be fitted on the bottom.

Most winters saw some cobles lost from Flamborough, so the fishermen started a Coble Club and Sick Fund to provide financial aid to build a new boat or help the families of anyone lost or who could not earn a living through illness. Fund raising took place on the last Saturday in June and was centred on a procession through the village led by the Flamborough Brass Band.

The introduction of engines made the cobles a lot safer, and the first engine was fitted to a Flamborough coble in 1920. At least one sailing coble was still working until about

1939 by which time the overall numbers were in decline. Gone were the days when cobles were packed on the slope at the North Landing either side of the track down past the winch hut and the lifeboat shed. By 1953 there were only eight cobles here and by 1982 this number had dropped to just Richard Emmerson's *Imperialist* and *Prosperity* and R. W. Emmerson's *Summer Rose* and *Spring Flower*.

Only the coble *North Star* and a few small boats were kept at the South Landing. However the North Landing boats were all active potting for crab on rocks towards Filey in the summer and carrying angling parties in the winter. When the weather permits, the cobles go out at 9 a.m. carrying parties of anglers. This is a major occupation on this stretch of the coast – one October Sunday in 1982 I counted forty-four boats, mostly Bridlington cobles with wheelhouses, anchored under the shelter of Flamborough Head with angling parties aboard.

Flamborough Head juts out into the North Sea dominating the coast and south of it the land slopes down to the lowlands of Holderness. This coast is lined with soft clay cliffs which crumble with every storm. The loss of land has been going on steadily for centuries and it is believed that since medieval times as many as thirty villages have gone into the sea and the coast has moved in around three miles. Certainly in the two small resort towns of Hornsea and Withernsea, very few houses are older than the nineteenth century, as the original towns of these names are out under the sea.

Hornsea had about six cobles working off the beach before World War I, but full-time fishing faded out here. In 1982 about twenty boats, a mixed bunch with some GRP cobles, were kept in a compound next to Hornsea amusement area. Most of these were being used for part-time fishing at the weekends. This was for crab potting in the summer and trammel netting in the winter for cod, whiting and skate.

Withernsea, in 1982, had four full-time boats and a few part-timers. The largest were the double-enders *Challenger II* and *Sea Horse* and the coble *Heike*. The sand on the beach is very soft and fishermen here use very powerful four wheel drive tractors to get the boat trolleys on to the slipway.

In effect Withernsea is the end of the coble coast although in the past cobles were sailed down to Yarmouth to take part in the autumn herring fishery. Some were sold south of the Humber, but were never really at home there. A few boats were used on Spurn Head by Norfolk fishermen who had migrated north before World War I.

One cannot leave this coast without mentioning the new beach landing at Aldbrough. Anglers used to manhandle their boats down the cliff face here. Every winter the sea ate away more brown clay cliff so that a new path had to be dug. The boat owners hit on the idea for sending the boats from the cliff top to the beach, about sixty feet below, on a wire. An engine is used to haul the boat up on the wire. Even then the cliff top hauling gear has to be moved back in the spring after the winter cliff subsidence. Wherever there is water, man finds a way of getting a boat on to it.

52

Chapter 4
The East Anglians

The coast of Eastern England between the River Humber and Eastern Kent is a land under siege. This coast has little rock to act as a natural breakwater and for centuries the sea has been slowly eating its way into the land. This erosion is made worse because this side of England is sinking. The coast and beaches on this coast are always shifting and changing because of the 'lateral drift' of tides. The land is eaten away in one place and piled up in another. In Viking and medieval times this coast had many small rivers, but many of their mouths have been choked by the silt deposited by lateral drift. In the nineteenth century, landowners started to protect their estates with modest coast defences, although most of these early sea defences were soon destroyed by storm damage.

The history of the East Coast is really a story of floods and erosion, with battles to stop much of Eastern England from becoming part of the seabed getting increasingly urgent. The most disastrous storm of modern times was at the end of January 1953. Westerly gales stopped the tide from escaping round Scotland and down the English Channel. The level of the North Sea rose and the sullen grey water simply rolled over the top of the inadequate sea defences. Much of the coast is now lined with groynes and concrete walls in attempts to prevent a repeat of the East Coast floods of 1953 and similar subsequent local high tides.

In medieval times the wool trade made this a prosperous and highly populated part of the country. There was a definite market for fish, but few good harbours until dredging began in the nineteenth century. It was easier to simply launch boats off the open beaches. Since there are few rocks or outcrops, boats could land virtually anywhere and Norfolk and Suffolk had more beach landings than most stretches of the coast.

The flat Lincolnshire coast has several silted-up river mouths, but the beaches here do not seem to have ever been great fishing centres. In the late nineteenth century, crab boats from Cromer and cobles from Yorkshire were used for whelking in Mablethorpe and the Grunnill family operated cobles from Skegness. In 1982 pleasure boats were kept on Skegness seafront, but there was little real beach work, as the coastal people had long looked to tourists from the industrial midlands, rather than the open sea, for an income. By 1878 the railways sometimes carried ten thousand trippers in a single day to the seafront of Cleethorpes (now in Humberside).

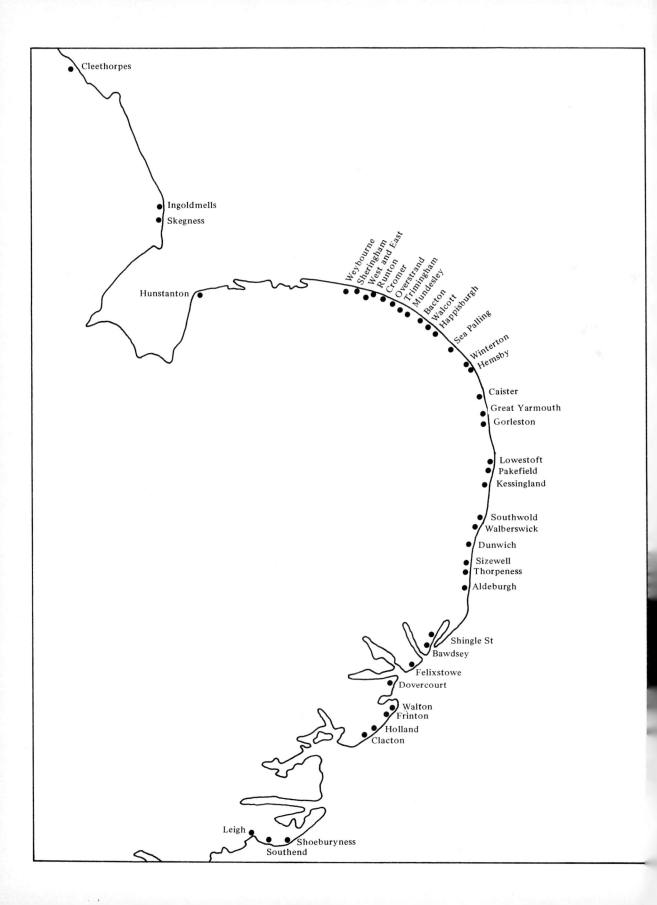

Cleethorpes

Ingoldmells
Skegness

Hunstanton

Weybourne
Sheringham
West and East
Runton
Cromer
Overstrand
Trimingham
Mundesley
Bacton
Walcott
Happisburgh

Sea Palling

Winterton
Hemsby

Caister
Great Yarmouth
Gorleston

Lowestoft
Pakefield
Kessingland

Southwold
Walberswick
Dunwich
Sizewell
Thorpeness
Aldeburgh

Shingle St
Bawdsey

Felixstowe
Dovercourt

Walton
Frinton
Holland
Clacton

Leigh
Shoeburyness
Southend

To the Victorian holiday maker, the piers at the seaside resorts were the major attraction. These once common sights are now slowly vanishing. Skegness lost its pier in a gale in 1978, although the thousand-seat pier end theatre still survives as a lonely island off the sandy beach. A new type of holiday for the masses was started in 1936 when at Ingoldmells, Billy Butlin opened his first holiday camp.

On the East Anglian coast, which stretches from the Wash to the Thames mouth, the railway age transformed numerous fishing hamlets into holiday resorts. In Norfolk the first of these was Hunstanton, where a branch line via King's Lynn to London was opened in 1862. In around 1900 there were two sailing boats, probably Yarmouth yolls, taking trippers off Hunstanton's flat sandy beach, but the true beach landings started at Sheringham.

In medieval times there was a headland called Shipden Ness just east of Sheringham. This has now completely eroded away, leaving rocky shoal water, but on the headland once stood the settlement of Shipden and its harbour. This harbour was finally engulfed by the sea in 1430 and the people moved to Cromer which had once been a village inland from Shipden. Even after the loss of the harbour the tradition of shipowning continued for another 500 years. In 1527 Cromer was sending thirty ships to fish and trade around Iceland, and Queen Elizabeth I granted the village the right to build a harbour in 1582. In fact a wooden jetty was built out on the beach so that ships could discharge cargoes. This jetty lasted about a century before being washed away in a storm. In 1845 a 240ft jetty was built and this lasted until 1897; but, with or without a jetty, Cromer was a port with vessels discharging their cargoes on the open beach.

The last few decades of Cromer's existence as a beach port are quite well recorded. In mid-Victorian times three traders, all schooners of about 80ft long, were engaged in bringing coal from the North of England. The normal practice was to run the schooner ashore at high tide and when the tide went down the horse-drawn tumbrils were taken out on the sand and filled with coal. When the cargoes were unloaded, the schooner floated and she was hauled off the beach by a hawser connected to an anchor which had been laid out when the schooner was put ashore.

This was a very slow process, because the schooners had to wait for settled weather before risking coming ashore. There are reports of Norfolk beach traders running into Yarmouth for shelter and then sailing back days later. It was reported that the *Mary Ann*, on passage from Hartlepool to beach at Mundesley, put into Lowestoft for shelter. She had gone some thirty miles past her destination. Another time, *Mary Ann* went into Yarmouth for shelter in December and it was reported that she returned to Mundesley to lay up for the winter.

The Cromer schooner *Ellis* was once caught on the beach by a sudden gale and driven right up to the cliff. She was left there all winter and the following spring was jacked up on to ways and relaunched back into the sea. Another time the Cromer schooner *Commerce* was badly damaged coming ashore on the beach in front of Sandford coalyard, which was on the cliff top beside the steep gangway leading down to the beach.

In most parts of Britain, beach landings existed only where there were suitable firm beaches. In Norfolk it would have been possible to put a ship ashore almost anywhere on the endless miles of sandy beach. So the Norfolk beach landings were sited where there was access for the tumbrils to get to the beaches. These places, where villagers brought in coal and exported corn were known as Gaps and some names still survive such as Trimingham Gap, Bacton Gap, Watch House Gap, Walcott Gap, Cart Gap and Horsey Gap. At Walcott Gap there was a capstan to help to haul the ships up the beach to give more time to discharge. Instead of having one horse on each tumbril, four horses were put on each one and the horses went out to the ship with the water up to their bellies.

The end of the beach trade came in 1877 when the Great Eastern Railway opened a line to Cromer; later a line was added to Mundesley. At the same time as the little cliff town of Cromer and its smaller neighbour, Sheringham, were fading out as trading ports, their offshore fishing fleet was also declining.

Although neither Cromer nor Sheringham had harbours, both had a fleet of 70ft fishing luggers known as the 'Great Boats'. Cromer had a long tradition of owning offshore fishing boats, and it is believed that the Upcher family encouraged and possibly even financed the Sheringham men into buying the 'Great Boats'. The Upchers had bought the Sheringham Estate in 1812 and for nearly a century did a great deal to

Norfolk crab boats at Cromer in about 1902. The men are filling ballast bags before going afloat   (Poppyland)

eliminate poverty and suffering in the little town. The 'Great Boats' went to the Yorkshire coast in the summer after crab, some of which were relaid off Cromer; in the autumn they drifted for herring out off Yarmouth, and then went long lining for cod in the winter. They only returned to Cromer and Sheringham a few times a year to land their gear for repair, and during the summer they were laid up at Morston or Yarmouth.

At the height of the 'Great Boat' fleet, around 1850, about forty luggers were owned in Sheringham, twelve in Cromer and a few in Runton and Overstrand. Since ten men were needed for the autumn 'herring voyage' they brought considerable employment into North Norfolk. The number of boats owned in Norfolk had fallen to forty in the 1860s and the last were sold in the 1890s. However, men from all the beach villages continued to go to Yarmouth and join the steam drifters. In the 1920s it was the practice on a Saturday, if the weather was fine, for the steam drifters to anchor off the coast so that the men could have a few hours ashore at home.

Although Cromer and Sheringham were both becoming holiday resorts in the late nineteenth century, there was still a lack of employment locally. One group of Norfolk men and their families were given free travel by rail, complete with crab boat, to go and settle in Grimsby. When the lifeboat station was closed at Grimsby in 1927 it was said that the entire crew were Sheringham men. Some more men went to Hornsea and others to Yorkshire beach landings. A fisherman called Mr Little moved to Felixstowe where his crab boats were a common sight until the 1950s. Perhaps the furthest place on the East Coast to which they went was Whitstable in Kent, where a Sheringham family moved to continue fishing. Off Cromer and Sheringham the patches of rough bottom are good ground for crabs and lobster, and working these has been the backbone of the North Norfolk fisheries for centuries. The Norfolk fishermen have a long but not always successful history of cooperating to try and preserve the crab stocks. In 1771 a society was formed to prevent the sale of small crab and to organise the crab sales to the London market.

In 1875 Frank Buckland, a fishing expert, prepared a Government report on summer crab and lobster fishing based at Weybourne, Sheringham, Runton and Cromer. Buckland reported about a hundred two man boats at Sheringham and fifty at Cromer. In all two hundred boats were working off the beaches of North Norfolk. This enquiry almost set off a local riot, because the Cromer men accused the Sheringham men of selling small crabs. It was many years before the friction between the two towns died down. However, the Crab and Fisheries Act of 1876 made it an offence to sell small crabs.

Until 1863 the hoop was used. This was simply an iron hoop supporting a net bag which had to be jerked from the bottom with the crab still feeding on the bait in it. The first crab pots were brought back by colliers returning from north-east England, but their efficiency probably helped to reduce local stocks. Fishermen also found ways to work more pots, so that in 1875 each boat worked 30 pots, but by 1905 some 109 North Norfolk boats were averaging 73 pots per boat. When engines were introduced in about 1923 the number of pots per boat rose to 110. These were all hauled by hand, very hard work, but when a small power capstan aft was introduced in 1967, the number of pots per boat rose again. By 1981 some Sheringham boats were working 200 pots.

Technology has not altered the sea conditions of Cromer beach. The double-ended crab boats which look like miniature Viking cargo ships and the Shetland model boats are probably true descendants of a Norse past. Now there is only one type of Norfolk crab boat, but in the nineteenth century half-decked 'pinkers' and the smaller half-decked 'hovellers' worked off the beaches. A 'hoveller' was a dialect term for a man (or his boat) who tended passing ships. They took out stores, replacements and anchors, or were engaged in salvage work. The hovellers went out of use when steam replaced sail in the merchant fleet.

By 1900 the hovellers' boats were being used for herring drifting and mackerel fishing. A removable deck forward made a cuddy where the men could shelter. This living accommodation, although very primitive, freed the hovellers from having to return to the beach every night. The last of the Cromer hovellers were Jimmy Davies' *James & Ellen* and Allen's *General Buller* which were going as far as Southwold, forty-five miles south, in 1930.

In about 1900 a Norfolk crab boat was sold to King's Lynn owners. This boat was much admired because of the basket-like qualities of the clinker hull. When the boat took the ground for cockling in the Wash the hull did not strain and leak like the carvel smacks which were not built to 'give'. Worfolk, the King's Lynn smackbuilder, built two new Lynn yolls, the *King Edward* and the *Baden Powell* for cockling based on the Norfolk crab boat at Lynn after World War II, but by 1982 there were only three Lynn cocklers going out working on the Wash banks.

The sail and oar crab boats were carried down the Norfolk beaches by oars pushed through 'orrucks' (oar locks) in the top plank. These oar holes were actually the same as those in the Viking longships. The oars were also used to control the boats coming ashore and having them in 'orrucks' meant that they were not thrown out at a critical stage. The beamy crab boats do roll in a big sea, but the floor boards are kept low to keep the weight down low. What the crab boats lose in speed they make up for in seaworthiness.

The problem with Sheringham and Cromer is that the top of the beach is steep shingle, and in a big sea the fishermen prefer to wait for the tide to ebb, and then land on the flat sandy foreshore. The aim is to bring a boat in at speed, staying on one sea, and then turn broadside just on grounding. The generous beam and pointed stern of the crab boat are very good for riding through the shallow waters before the beach is reached. Boats are sometimes swamped coming ashore, which is looked upon as being bad seamanship, although in a rising sea it is difficult to avoid this. A modern practice has been for the lifeboat to stand by.

At Cromer the boats are taken up on trailers pulled by old tractors. Only the east beach landing at Cromer is now used by the eight remaining crab boats and in bad weather they are parked in the steep gangway leading up the cliff. The west beach landing on the other side of the pier is now only used by angling and pleasure boats.

In 1982 there were only two boats left working full time from East End landing at Sheringham and three boats from the West End landing. The Sheringham West End has a steep concrete slip up which boats are hauled by motor winch. The East Enders usually leave their boats on the beach, but haul them up into an ally on a high tide. In March 1981 I witnessed this being done. It was raining and blowing hard and the little seaside town was deserted except for the East End where a cheerful crowd of fishermen were hauling the boats up with block and tackle. The tackle was made fast to an iron ring and five men ran up the road hauling while four put slides under the boat to steady the progress to safety.

Most of the crab boats built for engines are about 20ft long, the largest modern one being the 22footer at Cromer. The modern boats have straight stems to take the propeller, while the old sailing and oar boats had curved stern posts. Four generations of the Emery family of Sheringham built the Norfolk crab boats, but the modern ones like Eric Wink's 20ft *Mizpah*, built at Acle in 1968, mostly come from yards on the Norfolk Broads. In 1982 however, the *Original* was built at King's Lynn. The name means that she has a fine bow more like the original sailing 'Shannock' (the local nickname for Sheringham) boats.

The Norfolk crab boats have nearly all kept to petrol engines. It is believed that diesel is less reliable and would taint the whelks for which the boats were working off Blakeney in the winter. It was not until 1971 that any Norfolk boats were fitted with diesel engines.

The owner of *Joan Elizabeth* told me his boat had been built in 1973. He had fished in this type of boat for thirty years and his father and grandfather had used crab boats all their lives. There seemed no point in changing such a well-tried hull shape. The crab boat, either wooden or GRP, is still the only boat used by fishermen on the North Norfolk coast.

Crab boats being hauled up at the East End, Sheringham in 1981   (Jonathan Simper)

In 1982 there were crab boats kept at Sheringham, West and East Runton, Cromer, Overstrand and Happisburgh, although there were none at Trimingham, Mundesley or Bacton. The latter just had two old rusty hand winches with four ordinary open boats, while one GRP crab boat was kept behind the dunes at Cart Gap, Sea Palling.

Virtually all the villages between Sheringham and Yarmouth had a few boats before World War I. Jonathan Betts remembers that in about 1920 there were eleven boats kept at Overstrand and manned by twenty fishermen. In 1982 there were three boats kept here. The boats are kept down at the cliff foot and are only brought to the cliff top for maintenance or engine repairs. Jonathan Betts remembers that when a boat was moved on the beach it was done by eight men lifting oars through orrucks. The old men always insisted that the stern should come round 'with the sun' (clockwise). Betts and the younger men used to swing a boat with complete disregard for this ancient custom; however, if the older men caught them swinging a boat against the sun there was a great outburst of swearing.

Between June and September the practice with the sailing crab boats was to leave Overstrand beach about 8.30 p.m. and sail down to about Bacton where four packs of long lines were shot. The men then went ashore and 'dossed down' in the old barn at Happisburgh. This included men from Sheringham which was about twenty miles away. At around 3 a.m. they returned to sea to haul their lines at the break of day. On their way home they hauled up a 'couple of score' (40) of crab pots and rebaited them with 'rough stuff' from the long lines. Most of the bait for the lines had to be dug twelve miles away at Blakeney by the young men who travelled by bike.

The miles of golden sandy beach continue east of Happisburgh right down to Yarmouth, but here in the days of sail there used to be a different type of boat. Like the crab boats, these boats were double ended, clinker built and had single lug sails; but while the crab boats had rather fine shaped underwater lines these boats were virtually flat bottomed which resulted in them being known as punts. The beaches are generally flat on this lonely stretch of the coast so the boats were carried down to the water. At Hemsby, when the first holiday bungalows started to appear in the early 1920s, the dozen or so punts were still fishing from here.

From Hemsby south through Newport, California and Caister to Yarmouth is now a holiday land. These wonderful golden beaches have been claimed by the masses and are lined with miles of caravans and holiday camp sites. It is difficult to believe that this coast had some of the most lucrative beach boats in Britain. These were the famous East Anglian beach yawls which in the age of sail did so much salvage work on passing shipping. At its height in the mid-nineteenth century, hundreds of small merchant vessels passed close to this coast on passage to and from the North Country coal ports. These were constantly getting into difficulty and by the late eighteenth century men were using longshore fishing as a secondary occupation and forming themselves into 'beach companies' devoted to rescue and salvage. Each company had its headquarters and lookout post which was manned day and night. They took out supplies and spare anchors to ships, but their chief aim was to watch out for vessels in distress. Once a vessel was in trouble and was spotted, the beach yawls were hastily launched and under great lug sails they raced to be the first to reach their prey. The boats used were open double enders which, in print, were called yawls, but the East Anglians actually pronounced this as 'yoll' rather like the Scandinavian word jolle, meaning an open boat.

There were beach companies along some sixty-five miles of the coast from Happisburgh in Norfolk right down to Shingle Street in Suffolk. At Happisburgh (Haisbro to the locals), the beach yawls were kept down on the beach and the lifeboat on the top of the cliff. As the cliff has been eroded away the few Norfolk crab boats kept here have to be brought up a wooden roadway, and it is now difficult to believe that villages like this once had a large salvage company.

The next landing, Winterton, had two beach companies comprising sixty men in 1882. The coast is fairly clear of offshore banks so the Winterton men concentrated on pilot work. A century later the sea had receded so that the villages here are now inland behind high dunes and only a few pleasure boats are kept down near the beach.

The story is much the same at Caister: just a few pleasure boats where a century before there had been a salvage company supporting the village. The accounts of the Caister Company show the kind of returns that were being achieved. On average the yawls went out about twice a month in the winter. Sometimes the crews were rescued for no charge but if the vessel could be salvaged then a claim was made. For instance in April 1846 the yawls *Star* and *Wasp* refloated a brig and a schooner off the Scroby Sands. The company received £90 for the brig, but the schooner was loaded with wheat, so it earnt £123. At that time these combined amounts would have bought a new yawl. Even twenty-nine years later, in 1874, the hull of the Caister yawl *Zephyr II* was bought for £80.

One good salvage could pay for a new yawl, but it wasn't quite that simple because these highly specialised craft required an enormous number of men to operate them. Only about twenty men and the coxswain went out in the yawl, but when the company lookout spotted a ship in distress, the shout went out 'Running Down' and every member of the company and the families rushed to the beach to get their yawl afloat as quickly as possible. Both lives and incomes were at stake. The Caister Company had printed rules and one of the rules was that if a member touched any part of the boat during the launch, he received a share of the salvage. This often resulted in men who arrived late rushing into the water and touching the end of the mizzen outrigger of the departing yawl in order to claim their share.

Speed was the all-important quality of a yawl if it was to reach a ship in distress, either before it sank or before it was boarded by a rival company. The coxswain aft at the tiller had to be highly skilful in handling an open boat crashing through the rough seas. In these conditions the lee rail was often a foot below the surface, but the speed of the hull prevented the water from coming in. However, in the driving spray, part of the crew bailed out constantly; and some yawls were lost. In 1853 the three masted yawl *Increase*, owned by the Layton Company of Great Yarmouth, was returning from putting men aboard a brig in the Roads when she was suddenly caught aback (that is the wind on the leeward side of the sail). The pressure on the wrong side of the sail capsized the yawl at once and only one of the eight men aboard was saved.

In 1842 two yawls were lost from Sea Palling. The Companies here were called the Blues and the Whites because each one had their oars painted that colour so that their yawls could be distinguished at sea. The Palling yawls that were lost both capsized in the winter when going out to salvage. In the space of five weeks twelve men were lost, which must have been a terrible blow in a small remote coastal village. Considering the appalling conditions in which they usually went out, it is surprising that more yawls were not lost. Throughout the nineteenth century Lowestoft lost only three yawls.

Because of the herring fishery and the Yarmouth Roads anchorage, Great Yarmouth had the largest number of beach companies. It is likely that Yarmouth started as a fishermen's village in Saxon times. The great autumn 'Free Fair of Herring' was begun in 1270 and became a very important medieval trade fair. The mouth of the River Yare formed a haven, but this was mainly used by trading ships. Because of the difficulties of entering the shallow River Yare, almost all the fish was landed on the beach and taken overland to the curing houses. In good weather, the herring drifters ran ashore and discharged on the open beach. In bad weather, the drifters and the trawling smacks anchored in Yarmouth Roads and the beachmen, who used beamy yawls known as 'ferry boats', were employed to transport the catch ashore.

Yarmouth Roads are protected on the seaward side by the Scroby Sands, and ships have always come in here to shelter in bad weather. In the days of sail a North Sea gale saw perhaps four hundred ships arriving and some of these got into difficulty and needed help. In fine weather there was work for the ferry boats supplying the ships at anchor. There was also a naval station in these Roads. During the mid-nineteenth century the largest and most important beach landings in Britain were at Yarmouth Roads and The Downs in Kent.

Yarmouth Haven was constantly being improved, so that by 1867 most herring and mackerel from the drifters and the flat fish from the trawlers were landed over the quays. However the volume of small sailing ships in the coastal trade was enough to keep the beach companies busy. On Yarmouth beach there were the Standard, Diamond, Roberts, Denny, Holkham and Star companies while the Storm, Ranger and Young Flies Companies operated from Gorleston on the southern side of the Haven. Each company had a set of boats for different types of work, which included gigs and punts; but the beach yawls were the pride and big money earners of each company.

To launch off the flat beaches into shallow water, the yawls had to be shoal draught and were never fitted with centreboards. There was very little of the hull in the water and under a press of sail, the yawls kept upright by using moveable bags of shingle placed on the windward side. These long narrow yawls were the fastest working craft in Britain, and several achieved 14 knots while the 69ft Yarmouth three-masted *Reindeeer* once made 16 knots on a reach. In the summer the yawls raced for cash prizes in the coastal regattas. One of the largest of these must have been in 1888, when sixteen yawls with some four hundred beachmen aboard gathered at Yarmouth for the North Roads Regatta. By the 1890s the steamers, which were less inclined to get into trouble than the collier brigs and schooners, were rapidly taking over the trade, so that the beach companies began to decline.

The beach companies of Gorleston appear to have been the last to function on the east coast. The companies kept their boats actually inside the Haven at Brush Bend, and their headquarters overlooking the entrance are still standing. However, the appearance of these buildings has been altered. The Storm Company's headquarters is now the Storm House Cafe, although the lookout tower has recently been removed. The mainstay of the Gorleston Company's work was acting as unofficial pilots who helped with the extra work with ships entering and leaving port. The companies also maintained 'lifeboats' which were really their versions of the beach yawls. The three sheds where these lifeboats were housed, just above Brush Bend, were still standing in 1983. They are low brick buildings with pantile roofs and look strangely out of place in a quayside area which bustles with the activity of vessels supporting the North Sea drilling rigs.

What is more surprising is that one of the beach companies' lifeboats is still afloat as a motor cruiser in the Norfolk Broads. This is the *Friends of All Nations* (FOAN for short) which was built in 1862 and was housed in the Rangers shed until 1880. The beach company's lifeboat *Elizabeth Simpson*, built in 1889, is still in service as a pleasure boat and other boats to survive from before World War I are the pleasure 'yolls' which were gaff sloops and ran trips off Yarmouth beach in the summer.

The largest of the Yarmouth pleasure yolls was the 42ft *Britannia*, but those that survive include the *Caister Maid*, the 31ft *Edward Birbeck* built in 1896, and the 37ft *Amity* built in 1912. The *Amity* does not have the famous 'Yarmouth hump', a rise in the sheer just aft of the bow, which was supposed to stop the water coming aboard as they were launched. The Yarmouth hump was used in fishing boats and beach yawls and might have been developed from the coble bow. Yorkshire cobles used to come down for the autumn herring fishery and cobles were being used on Yarmouth beach until at least the 1850s. By the time *Amity* was built, the coble and the hump were out of fashion, but the Norfolk men knew how to build a clinker double-ended hull with a good all round sailing performance. The *Amity* was built for the Butoger brothers and was damaged on Yarmouth beach when the German Navy shelled the town during World War I. After this she became a Brancaster fishing boat and then a yacht. The next generation of beach boats at Yarmouth broke completely with tradition and were basically just motor launches. In the early 1920s there were twenty-eight of this type used for pleasure boating and going after herring and mackerel. There were also about forty beach skiffs, clinker transom sterned boats, which were always rowed but were used for the same purposes.

The number of boats working off Yarmouth beach stayed at about twenty-eight until World War II. These boats were licenced to carry twelve passengers, but by 1950 eleven boats were averaging about twenty-two passengers so that the trend was towards fewer but larger boats concentrating on pleasure trips. Another perhaps rather obvious move was for boats to be kept in the Haven and the last boat left Yarmouth beach in 1972. Pleasure trips continued from the beach by David Wells' *Glenda Margaret* and another boat.

Eight miles south of Yarmouth is the rival port of Lowestoft. The beach at Lowestoft is now a mass of concrete sea defences and it would be impractical to keep a working boat there. However, it was an important beach landing for centuries. The original Saxon settlement in this area was at Oulton, some two miles inland. In the dark centuries when Vikings and other pirates followed the coast looking for places to raid, it was advisable to be tucked away inland out of sight. The Oulton settlement was linked to Lowestoft beach by a track, later known as Fisher Row, but by medieval times there was a small town on the high ground above the beach beside a silted-up estuary. In about 1770 a community had grown up near The Beach, which was separated by poverty and a cliff from the rest of Lowestoft. By the late eighteenth century Lowestoft

63

The Norfolk yoll *Amity* sailing as a cruising yacht, 1980   (Author)

was a thriving beach landing, particularly in the autumn when herring came in from deep water to spawn in shallow water along the East Anglian coast. The boats used were decked, three-masted luggers of about 40ft. In 1831 a harbour was opened at Lowestoft and this triggered off the expansion of the town as a major fishing centre. However, although new docks were built, many of the small fishermen's homes remained in the Beach Village. In fine weather, the luggers continued to discharge into horse and cart on the open beaches; and it was not until the arrival of steam tugs that it became quicker for the sailing drifters to go into the harbour.

Beach companies or simple groups of beachmen co-operating for mutual benefit had probably existed on the east coast from Elizabethan times, but it was not until the late eighteenth century that a clear picture of the Lowestoft beach companies emerges. Lowestoft's North and South Roads are not quite as favourable anchorages as Yarmouth Roads, but they were still good enough to shelter large fleets. In the early and middle nineteenth century it was quite normal for fleets of about five hundred ships to make a passage along the east coast in favourable weather from one anchorage to the next.

In the 1780s Lowestoft men in their 'yolls' (yawls) were busy putting pilots aboard passing ships, Joseph Denny's South End Company organized its 'court' (headquarters where the men met), gear store and lookout tower just near Lowestoft Ness. By 1835 there were three informal beach companies operating off Lowestoft beach and it was

64

decided to constitute them into a properly organized footing. Denny's Company became the Old Company, while Reads and Lincolns became the Young Company. This arrangement does not seem to have pleased all the beachmen, because two years later a new company, the North Road Company, was set up. After about thirty years the North Road Company more or less joined up with the Young Company. However in 1881 there were 279 people who were shareholders in the Lowestoft Companies, some of whom would have been widows and dependants.

The beachmen had an unwritten rule that whichever company's yawl reached a distressed vessel first, they could claim that salvage. When the lifeboat started going to vessels in distress, even after the yawl's crew had boarded them, there were some very angry scenes. It took the beachmen quite a while to accept the fact that the lifeboat's only job was to save lives, and that they were not a rival beach company. They were even more annoyed when the steam tugs gradually took over more and more of the lucrative salvage work.

By the 1890s the beach yawls were mainly being kept for racing and were only occasionally launched to a salvage. The races increased the rivalry between beach companies and there was constant striving to produce the fastest yawl. In 1853 the Young Company abandoned the three-masted yawl when they built the *Mosquito*, the first two-master. She was named after a famous racing yacht of the time, so there is no doubt what influenced the beachmen. In 1892 the Young Company were forced to withdraw from racing because the yawl *Young Prince* was worn out. A group of

The Lowestoft beach yawl *Happy New Year* leaving harbour, probably with a racing crew aboard (Author's Collection)

gentlemen clubbed together and raised the money to build the 48ft *Georgiana*, which must rank as the fastest yawl built. Rivalry was strong, as the Old Company promptly commissioned George Watson, then one of the world's leading yacht designers, to design a fast yawl. The result was the 50ft *Happy New Year* (a name used for several of the company's yawls) which was built in 1894. The *Happy New Year* and *Jubilee*, also designed by Watson, never really equalled the *Georgiana*, which had been designed by a Lowestoft man called Capps.

By the time the last yawl race was sailed at Lowestoft in 1907, the *Georgiana* had taken fifteen firsts. Within a few years most of the beach companies had ceased to operate and their beloved yawls were left to decay on the open beaches. By the mid-1920s the beach yawls were already a thing of the past. However, the Norfolk and Suffolk type lifeboats were giving good service for another half century. Only on the stretch of coast between Caister and Aldeburgh did the working boat type influence the RNLI lifeboat. The world's first sailing lifeboat was built in 1807 and was based at Lowestoft. This lifeboat, *Frances Ann*, was built to the design of the London coachbuilder, Lionel Lukin, who had spent a holiday at Lowestoft. Lukin spent a lot of time talking to beachmen and based his boat design on their yawls.

The Norfolk and Suffolk lifeboats remained very similar to the yawls and continued as sailing boats because with so many shipwrecks taking place on sandbanks miles off the coast, the lifeboat had to cover long distances which were too slow and exhausting under oar only. As more lifeboats were stationed on the East Anglian Coast, the sailing qualities became less important, because when a rescue was needed the nearest lifeboat to windward was called out and she simply ran down wind. When the 44ft RNLI Norfolk and Suffolk lifeboat *Alfred Corry* was built at Lowestoft in 1893, she was given a very beamy clinker hull, but although she had a cork fender round her, the *Alfred Corry* was still clearly a cousin of the beach yawl. The *Alfred Corry* was built mainly to the suggestions of the Southwold coxswain and longshore fisherman John Cragie. This lifeboat was on the Southwold station for twenty-five years and then became a yacht and finally a houseboat at Maldon, Essex. It was here in 1977 that John Cragie, Essex rivers pilot and grandson of the original coxswain, discovered her in a very dilapidated state but as the hull was still in good order he had her converted to a gaff ketch yacht and she is back sailing under her original name.

There are no longer any beach boats at Lowestoft and the nearest landing is the shingle beach at Pakefield, about one and a half miles south of the harbour. In 1882 Pakefield beach company had seventy members and in the early 1900s it raced the yawl *Sir Savill Crossley*. Now the village has become part of urban Lowestoft and has about fifty boats used for angling and part-time fishing on the beach. Four of the old bar capstans are still in use. These are just plain wooden drums mounted on boards and turned by a bar inserted through a hole in the top. It was possible for a couple of men to pull up a 15–19ft boat with one of these. However, for large boats and yawls the long vanished 'crab capstans' were used, which were upright drums turned by pushing on a bar, but they were larger and mounted on a framework supported by three legs. In some cases the legs were curved so that it looked a bit like a crab. In 1982 I spoke to a retired shipwright who said that he could remember the *Georgiana* being hauled up by chain on Lowestoft North beach by a horse operating a crab capstan.

66

Pakefield is really the beginning of the homeland of the Suffolk beach boat. These are a clinker-hulled open boat with a transom stern, usually about 20ft long. In the few paintings and drawings of the Suffolk coast before about 1815, the boats on the beaches appear to be double-ended, but still seem to have been much more flat-bottomed than the Norfolk crab boats. These flat bottoms caused the sailing versions to be known as punts and it also allowed them to be great bulk carriers which was important when trying to land vast quantities of sprat and herring. In the 'Aquatic Sports' at Lowestoft in 1860 there was a race for 'lug-sailed' beach boats and in the Kirkley and Pakefield Regatta there were classes for 18ft and 16ft punts, so that the type was in common use by then.

These beach boat regattas were once very keenly fought local affairs. The last one appears to have been held at Kessingland ('Kess'el to the locals), as late as 1948. The Kessingland beach is only some five miles from Lowestoft and many of the beachmen spent part of the year in the steam drifters. Successful owners moved to live in the village. One Kessingland owned steam drifter was the *Result* which earned fame by rescuing the crew of another steam drifter while the fleet was working from Lerwick.

Alice Maud being hauled out at Kessingland in 1957. The *Alice Maud* was built as a sailing punt in 1884. At this stage she was fitted with a 7 hp car engine. Like all Suffolk punts an extra plank has been added because the engine pulled them down lower in the water   (Fishing News)

The beach boat *Result* built in 1936, the last to be built in Kessingland, was named after the famed drifter. In 1982 she was owned by seventy-five year old Stanley 'Cock Robin' Brown who still used her for part-time fishing, while most of the other thirty or so boats on the beach were used for angling.

'Cock Robin' Brown remembers that in the early 1920s there were twenty-eight punts working from Kessingland which at peak times employed some sixty men. These longshore punts from Pakefield and Kessingland concentrated on sprat because the Lowestoft drifters were flooding the markets with herring. However, they had to follow the seasonal fishing pattern and in late October they went out in beach skiffs with herring drift nets. Once the herring shoals were known to have arrived, they started taking out the larger sailing punts, but even then they did not go unless the price was right. It was a waste of time to glut the market. If there was a good market the punts went eight miles up the coast on the flood tide to Southwold and then drifted back on the tide. Hopefully each punt found the shoals. Sometimes they met Lowestoft harbour boats which had taken so many herring that they could not empty their nets. At least one Lowestoft boat sank off Kessingland because she had been overloaded with herring, and a Kessingland punt picked up all the crew.

The autumn sprat and herring fishery was the Suffolk beachmen's harvest; it was their main income. Off Kessingland the North Sea is rather shallow, particularly near Benacre Ness, which seems to have restricted the amount of trawling. Instead, in the summer, they went after salmon. By the 1930s many of the local men could not make a living off the beach and the number of boats started to drop. However, by 1937, some of the drudgery started to go out of their lives when the first motor winches replaced the bar capstans.

During the 1930s fishing communities were still very close-knit and the families tended to stick to fishing so that there were several fishermen with the same surnames. To overcome this, the nickname, which often originated in the school playground, was used widely. Apart from 'Cock Robin' at Kessingland, another member of the Brown family was 'Hurricane' Brown. In 1948 'Hurricane' had the 18ft 6in long, 7ft 9in beam, 18in draft *Valsand* built by Frank Fuller on the North Beach, Lowestoft. The name *Valsand* was derived from the owners two daughters' names, Valerie and Sandra. This custom of making up a name from a family was then a fairly recent invention, but fishing boats had long had homely names. The terms 'boy' or 'girl' in front of a name was a widely used custom which followed Suffolk dialect usage.

The *Valsand* was used for long lining, spratting, herring and mackerel drifting, shrimping and trawling. Landing a boat on a beach daily is very demanding on a hull and the Suffolk beach boat men needed to change their boats about every ten years. The usual practice was to sell them to owners in the harbours or estuaries. In 1981 the *Valsand* was in Southwold harbour which was the base of twenty full-time inshore fishing boats. Only one fishing boat and a few angling craft were kept on the beach in front of the town, but this was once an important beach landing.

The harbour at Southwold was badly silted up in Victorian times, so the beach was used. At the same period the sailing vessels came in and sheltered off Southwold. The anchorage here was never used on the same scale as Yarmouth or even Lowestoft, but there was enough work for Southwold to have beach companies. The Kilcock Cliff

Company, which had its headquarters on the hill top approximately where the Sailor's Reading Room is, was the main company. Also there was the Klondike Company operating from near the pier, and at the bottom of Gun Hill there was the California Company. These two companies may have been just informal groups, because some sources refer to them as the Long Island Company and the New York Cliff Company. At any rate North America figured prominently in the imaginations of the Southwold beachmen.

A tombstone dated 1786 in Southwold churchyard shows a three masted lugger with a clinker hull, which presumably was a forerunner of the beach yawl. Between 1846–70 James Critten is reputed to have built six beach yawls at Southwold. The Crittens seem to have concentrated on building beach punts later on so that when Kilcock Cliff Company wanted a new yawl in 1892, they got Beeching Bros of Yarmouth to build it. The result was the 48ft *Bittern* which was the last of the Southwold yawls and in the early 1920s was still used with the yawl *John Bull* to recover anchors. The *Bittern* was eventually presented to Southwold as a memorial to the town's beachmen. No steps were taken to preserve her and she was just left on the North Beach where in 1929 her decayed hull was finally broken up. The rudder of the *Bittern* was saved and now stands outside the Sailors Reading Room, virtually all that remains of a true beach yawl.

The beach fishing fleets expanded when the railway reached Southwold in 1879, which led to herring, sprat, smelt, shrimp, sole and cod being sent to London. These boats had three hands for drifting and two for trawling. In the summer a day's trawling

Three generations of the Critten family, boat builders on the north beach, Southwold   (John Cragie)

The 44ft double-ended Norfolk and Suffolk lifeboat *Alfred Corry* being launched into a whole gale from the south beach at Southwold, 1896. Note the 'setts' or pushing poles and the hauling off warp   (John Cragie)

was often lost because there was not enough wind. To overcome this some enterprising fishermen invented the unique drawsail. This was a square of canvas with a pole along the top which was put in the water in front of the bows and this pulled the boat along at the speed of the tide.

Another Southwold invention was a leeboard, in the form of a board being put down on the leeward side to help sail against the wind. Over the bar at the 'Bell' at Walberswick is some of the sailing gear, including the leeboard of the punt *Smiling Morn*. She was built by Critten in 1903 and given a gaff sloop rig for running trips off the beach. When Billy 'Barr' Stannard bought her he converted her to the lug rig for fishing. The nickname 'Barr' came from the American yacht skipper Barr and was given to him because he won the coveted Elms Cup, a trophy all the Suffolk punts raced for. Barr Stannard fished as far south as Woodbridge Haven (River Deben) and his racing reputation led the Aldeburgh men to invite him to their race in the hope of beating a Thorpeness punt which had been monopolising their race.

On the morning Barr went down to the harbour to sail the ten miles to Aldeburgh, he found that rivals had smashed off the rudder pintles so that he could not use that boat. The gear was hurriedly transferred to the *James & Charles*, a punt he had just bought from Pakefield, and they set out. When his son 'Ernie' Stannard related the incident nearly sixty years later, he described the sea as breaking 'steeple deep' as they left

70

Southwold harbour. Off Aldeburgh the race was round a triangular course and 'Barr' gained time by swinging the lug round in front of the mast instead of dipping it aft of the mast. But this could only be done when the wind was light. When the wind freshened the other boats lost time reefing, but 'Barr' carried on with full lug sail and won the race.

Just before World War I Southwold had serious trouble with coastal erosion and by the 1920s most of the beach was taken up with sea defences. Motors were also introduced so that working out of the harbour was no longer a problem. The beachmen from Southwold, and a few on the Walberswick shore, moved their capstans to the harbour and worked from there. After a time stages were built and the boats did not have to be hauled out any more. In about 1927 when Billy English of Walberswick wanted to start fishing on his own he joined a Lowestoft drifter to amass enough capital to buy a boat. After sixteen weeks away he returned home and bought the 18ft *Maud Ellen* for £8 complete with trawl and shrimp trawl.

Drift nets which had been used for one season by the Lowestoft drifters were bought and cut down. The usual practice was to drift along the shore with one end of the net almost in the breakers and often they averaged about seven to eight thousand herring a night. These herring were sold in a pattern that can be traced back to medieval times. A 'warp' was four herring, a 'short hundred' was a hundred herring and a 'long hundred' was one hundred and thirty-six herring. The way of calculating the long hundred was also complex. The fishermen held two herrings in each hand which they called 'long tailed herring'. They then counted two handfuls thirty-four times so that the 'long hundred' was reached. This method of selling survived in the beach landings after Yarmouth and Lowestoft fish markets had gone over to the cran (basket) measure.

One summer's day in the late 1920s Billy English counted eighty-seven longshore boats trawling off Southwold. The depression which started in 1929 depleted this fleet considerably. During World War II Southwold harbour was closed so that it could not be used by invading forces. About twenty boats returned to fishing off Southwold beach, but they took to the harbour once the war was over. In 1948 the 16ft punt *Faith*, built by Critten, was bought by Mr Winter and was worked by him with his son John Winter under sail. The *Faith* was one of nine boats which were swept up the harbour and smashed to pieces on the bridge in the 1953 floods. Later several more of the old sailing punts were deliberately destroyed so that their owners could claim flood compensation.

After Southwold, which sits on high ground, the Suffolk coast sweeps in to form Dunwich Bay. The soft sandy cliffs of Minsmere and Dunwich have over the centuries been considerably eroded away and the old medieval town of Dunwich which sent ships to the Icelandic fishery and was a major religious centre in East Anglia, is now under the sea. This once active port had in the past century only a few boats working off the shingle beach. In 1980 only one of these, *Dingle Bight*, was working full time. The year before this at Dunwich there had been a problem which periodically affects many beach boats. One was swamped when coming ashore and it had to have the engine completely stripped down.

From the sea the coast after Minsmere is dominated by the huge nuclear power station. This uses the seawater for cooling the reactors, which puts the temperature of the sea up enough to increase fish stocks. Since the power station was built in the 1950s the number of boats kept here has increased, but these are worked part time. Some of

Right
Southwold beach fisherman
clearing sprat out of his net.
The job of shaking out the
drift net was a long and
laborious task
(Suffolk Photo Survey)

Left
Roger Smith's *Kingfisher*
caught on a groyne at
Southwold in 1947 due to
thick fog. She was a beamier
version of Palmer's *Arthur &
Phyllis* and survived this
mishap to be smashed up in
the 1953 floods. Note the
'galley pump' on the starboard
quarter which was a usual
form of Southwold bilge pump
(Doreen Cragie)

the old bar capstans still lie on the beach but the first motor was fitted to a winch at Sizewell in 1950. This cost the owner £8 but it was destroyed in the 1953 floods. The winch that is still working was paid for with the £25 compensation. Sizewell beach in 1982 with its little collection of boats was incredibly peaceful, yet a bitter national debate was taking place about whether to build Sizewell B, an extension to the power station, part of the controversy over how Britain should produce power in the future.

After Sizewell the sea becomes very shallow off Thorpeness. In 1910 the sea burst through to flood the marshes south of the hamlet of Thorpe. This was part of the estate of the barrister and dramatist Glencairn Stuart Ogilvie, who was inspired to create a holiday village around a lake. Ogilvie had the boating mere dug in 1911 and until 1930 continued to develop the renamed Thorpeness as a unique holiday village of mock Tudor houses.

Before World War I Thorpeness had fourteen full-time fishermen. Sometimes a bank would build up off the beach, making landing difficult. At such times the fishermen loaded their crab capstans up into their punts and moved round to Sizewell for a time. If the fishing was poor off this section of the coast, then the Thorpeness men loaded up their punts again and sailed some eleven miles south round Orford Ness and established themselves on Shingle Street beach. The large punts were put ashore and the men lived under these while working the smaller punts. To sell their catch, they sailed up the River Deben to supply Woodbridge.

In 1976 Henry Harling, a Thorpeness fisherman who was then over ninety, told me how he had a boat for each type of fishing. The 21ft *Gypsy Queen* was for trawling and the 18ft *Industry* was a lighter boat for rowing along the shore with herring drift nets. These were punts with two-masted lug rig, but his 14ft beach skiff was just for rowing off to the lobster pots on the 'Rocks'. The limitation of sail and oar meant that they seldom went further than three miles off the beach. In the 1920s Henry Harling and Percy Westrup fitted engines into their boats for trawling. Westrup's boat was the 18ft *Three Sisters*, built in 1896 of oak planks on oak frames. This was typical of these beach boats, because oak was a common tree in East Suffolk.

The Thorpeness fishermen gradually found it easier to get a living by working in the holiday village than from the uncertain returns of longshore fishing. Westrup's punt finished up abandoned on the River Ore and I tried to buy her for restoration as she was the only genuine 18ft sailing Suffolk punt left. The owner would not part with her, but curiosity drew me back to Thorpeness where I purchased a smaller but equally dilapidated punt, the 15ft *Pet*.

This boat was one of a number built at the turn of the century at Sudbourne, an inland village, by a wheelwright called Bugg. The *Pet* first appears on the register in 1902 as belonging to a Thorpeness man. In her long career she was moved around a great deal, going first to Aldeburgh and then to Southwold in 1922, where she was rebuilt and had another plank added to the hull; then back to Thorpeness before being sold to a Lowestoft owner. In 1930 she was rowed by 'Keydie' Wilson and another fisherman from Lowestoft the thirty miles to Aldeburgh. One of the Cable family, who had a fish shop in the High Street, worked *Pet* off Aldeburgh beach until 1937 when she returned to Thorpeness, to be worked by George Wilson. The *Pet* must have been the last fishing boat in East Anglian to work under sail, for right up to 1957 Wilson sailed out to his lobster pots. After this an outboard was fitted.

Wilson died in 1964 and the *Pet* was left on the beach, being used less and less. She was not safe to go out in when we bought her, but enough of the hull was sound for Frank Knight's boatyard at Woodbridge to rebuild her in 1981. Some of the smaller punts had just a single mast, but we found traces of a mizzen in *Pet*, and she was therefore refitted as a two masted lugger. We had never sailed a dipping lugger and on the first attempt had very little control over the boat, but in time and after talking to several fishermen it proved to be a fast rig and sailed closer to the wind than a gaff sail.

The *Pet*'s other means of propulsion, the heavy oars worked in throles, we lacked enthusiasm to try; but these proved very effective and in spite of her size she slipped through the water well. The next stage was to fish under sail. The lug sail with reasonable wind does develop enough power to tow a small beam trawl but the real success was in working herring drift nets. Like all traditional craft she was evolved to suit a particular function. There is plenty of space aft to stand on a flat bottom and haul nets. Between the thwarts on either side of the hull are the 'wings' (fish compartments) which kept the catch out of the working space and the weight distributed evenly. The general conclusion is that if you only had wind and muscle power, this type of craft was a very good working platform for longshore fishing.

The Thorpeness men found boats the size of *Pet* very handy for going out to a patch of rough bottom, The Rocks, where the lobsters thrived. In the nineteenth century this kept men employed during some of the summer. One of the men would periodically sail with the combined catch the twenty-five miles to Harwich and sell them to Denny, a fish merchant. The drawback with Thorpeness is that it is exposed and the men often had to land at Sizewell or Aldeburgh and walk home.

In 1983 Aldeburgh had the largest fleet of any beach landing in East Anglia. Aldeburgh with its off-lying shallows creating short breaking seas can be very dangerous for landing, but a map of 1588 in the reign of Queen Elizabeth I, clearly shows boats and crab capstans on the beach, so the beach fishery appears to have been long established even then.

Herring and sprat have been one backbone of the Aldeburgh fishing in the autumn since medieval times. In Elizabeth I's reign three hundred fishermen were said to have taken part in the 'Spratte Fare' and in the Victorian era two hundred men came home for the autumn season. Many went away in the summer as paid crew on large yachts. Traditionally Aldeburgh sent the first of the season's sprats as a gift to London for the Lord Mayor's Banquet. The town was anxious to get all the publicity it could for its main product, and in about 1904 there was an attempt to develop a Sprat Feast along the lines of the Colchester Oyster Feast, but this did not last long.

Sprats were caught in large numbers and punts were loaded down so that the water was within a few inches of the top plank. When Billy Burrell first went fishing in 1938, engines had only been fitted into the Aldeburgh boats for a few seasons and it was the custom to take them out in the sprat season so that the boats could load more. In addition, if a boat was swamped coming ashore, at least the engine was not ruined. Money values have changed completely since the 1930s, because if a man could earn over £1 a week then he was doing well.

In 1948 two lorry loads and two railway truck loads of sprat in boxes were sent away every fine day during the season. The largest haul that Billy Burrell landed was 4" tons of sprat in his 19ft *Girl Lu*. In the following three decades there was a complete change in the pattern of Aldeburgh fishing. There is little demand for sprat now, and instead they only land them for bait and to sell from their huts on the beach. In the past the sea off Aldeburgh was only fished by Aldeburgh boats, but due to the introduction of powerful engines, longshore boats from Lowestoft, Southwold and Harwich can reach these waters.

The introduction of the engine has shortened the working hours ashore and afloat, and the types of boat have altered. The sailing punts had fine lines so the hull slipped through the water with minimum effort, but diesel engines can push a hull easily so these boats are now much fuller in bow and stern. This gives more working space and the wide bows (some men call them 'bulldog bows') give more space to stand in for working

Colin Smith's *Dorothy May* returning to Aldeburgh from longlining in 1981. The Aldeburgh boats work to the north of the landing   (Author)

the longlines. Cars mean that fishermen no longer have to live within walking distance of the beach. In 1983 about thirty men were working some twenty boats off Aldeburgh beach but only six men were from the long-established fishing families. Many of the other men did not even live in Aldeburgh, but drove in daily from the surrounding villages. This state of affairs was rather forced on the fishermen because the town, largely due to its music festival, has a large number of 'holiday' or 'second homes' which has forced local people away from the attractive streets where they once lived.

On Aldeburgh seafront there are two Victorian brick towers which were built by the 'Up-Town' and 'Down-Town' pilots associations. These were basically beach companies, but Aldeburgh was also a convenient place for vessels coming in from the North Sea to pick up a pilot for the Thames Estuary. Before World War I the pilot station was moved to Harwich and one tower is now a holiday home while the other is used by the RNLI.

Sometimes, when after dogfish, the Aldeburgh boats work up to 12 miles offshore, which is a long way if the wind suddenly rises. On 10 April 1972 the men judged the weather to be settled enough to put to sea at first light, but hardly had they got out when a Force 7 gale from the SSE started to rise. By 10 a.m. everyone was ashore safely except the 18ft *Ocean Pride* with three men aboard.

The Aldeburgh lifeboat was launched into a very angry sea with heavy rain squalls bringing visibility down to 250 yards. The *Ocean Pride* was located about a mile south of Aldeburgh coming back in a wild sea with the wind then gusting Force 9. The beach

76

boat coped with the huge seas well and crossed the outer shoal safely, but as she passed over the inner shoal a huge white foaming sea threw her skywards and then as she sank into the next trough the steep sea broke over the boat and she went down. Two men were got out on to the lifeboat quickly and then the coxswain, Reuben Wood, took the lifeboat stern first into the breakers and they just managed to save the third man before he was overcome with the cold.

The difficulties of working off an open beach can never be underestimated and it is hardly surprising that many beach landings were abandoned for full time fishing when alternative sources of employment became available. However the two beach landings south of Aldeburgh, Shingle Street and Bawdsey, seem to have been abandoned because before World War II the fishermen could not find a wide enough market for their catch. The hamlet of Shingle Street probably did not exist before 1810 when the building of the Martello Towers created a settlement. The original houses were just single storey cottages built by squatters from driftwood. Beachcombing (locally 'shoreing') in the age of wooden ships was a fruitful occupation for the wives, (and in bad weather for the fishermen) on the Suffolk coast. Shingle Street's only link with the outside world was a track along the beach to Bawdsey. Later on a road was constructed across the marshes so that fresh water could be taken daily from Hollesley. The Shingle Street people lived an incredibly independent life with little contact with neighbouring villages. By fishing,

The Thorpeness punt *Pet* off the Landmark beach, Bawdsey. These punts were evolved for working off the steep Suffolk shingle beaches. The Norfolk crab boats worked off flat shallow beaches which had totally different conditions   (Author)

wildfowling, poaching and beachcombing they managed to survive. Necessity being the mother of invention, Shingle Street men devised a huge underwater spoon which they worked from their boats to get coal out of the ships sunk off Orfordness.

In Victorian times the Bawdsey fishermen landed on the north side of East Lane point, but this land and the coastguard cottages on it was eroded away, so the landing was moved to the Landmark on Bawdsey cliff. Like Shingle Street men the Bawdsey men had to do other work to make a living. 'Iky' Ford was marshman looking after cattle, while 'Taler' Friend did some shoemaking. 'Taler' got his name because he was born in the Martello tower where the family had moved after the father was turned out of the village for poaching on the Bawdsey Estate.

The Bawdsey men had the same problem as hundreds of other beachmen working from isolated landings in that even when the catch was good the local demand was not enough to sell everything. Fortunately for Bawdsey men, they could cross the Deben Ferry and walk about four miles to get their catch on the railway to Billingsgate where 'East Lane Welks' were sold under that name. When some of the men returned from fighting in World War I they used their gratuity to buy new boats and gear. In the 1920s there were five men working single masted Suffolk punts at the Landmark, but once engines were available the fishing centre shifted to the River Deben because even with its dangerous entrance it was still easier than working off the open beach.

The Bawdsey landing finally petered out when during World War II all the east coast beaches were mined and lined with anti-invasion defences. As a boy, just after the war, I often went to the shingle beach at Bawdsey Landmark, but it was quite empty except for a lone iron winch which has now vanished. The Ford family still lived in the village, but were working a pleasure boat off the Dip, over the Deben at Felixstowe. Henry Beeton and some other Shingle Street men had keenly revived part time trawling off their beach, while some of my first times afloat were trawling in the *Lassie*, which was reputed to have been built as a Shingle Street beach boat with an engine, but the beach at East Lane remained deserted until some anglers placed a winch there in 1980 and started keeping boats there again.

The town of Felixstowe did not exist before the railway reached here from Ipswich in 1874. It is a common mistake to think that new towns are found only in North America, Australia and other new countries, because many of the coastal resorts round Britain are much younger than some of the cities on the east coast of the United States. Felixstowe, Walton, Frinton, Clacton and even Southend are just some of the new towns round the coast of East Anglia, and their creation led to the establishment of new beach landings.

Views of Felixstowe in the 1890s show one rowing boat taking visitors out for trips. By 1910 there were four tripper boats and trips off the beach became one of the main attractions of Felixstowe. In the 1930s the Newsons of Felixstowe Ferry commissioned W. H. Blake to design the *Deben Viking* which ran trips up the River Deben and the *Orwell Viking* which ran trips up the River Orwell. These were decked craft which were kept in the River Deben but operated off Felixstowe beach. Only the *Deben Viking* survived World War II, but in the late 1940s the tripper trade boomed again because the public had not been able to go on the sea for several years. Launches ran from The Dip, the Fludyers Hotel and to the north of the pier, taking people out to the Cork lightship. In fine weather they could actually board the Cork and the visit was made more popular

The new tripper boat *Vanguard* at Cann's Gas House Creek yard, Harwich. She was built for Southend and was the final development of the East Anglian beach yawl   (Mark Richmond)

by a hat being passed round for a tip for the lightship men. The demand for this type of trip faded away so that by the mid-1960s the Felixstowe tripper boats had ceased to operate.

On the Essex coast, the resorts in Tendring Hundred were created by the railways in the late nineteenth century. Walton-on-the-Naze had open lug and spritsail boats which were used in the summer for lobstering in the mornings, and were then scrubbed down for passenger trips in the afternoons. Some of the Cook family ran pleasure boats off the South Beach at Lowestoft, and they moved to Frinton-on-Sea to operate pleasure boats and bathing machines on the seafront. Much of the road making material for building the new town of Clacton-on-Sea was actually discharged on the open beach. Sailing barges went ashore at Clacton Wash with Kentish rag stone and discharged into horse and cart in one tide. There were also men with open boats taking trippers out. In between this work they went fishing with 4ft hoop nets for dab, and they also went after whiting. In the winter they used to row out to the Colne and Tollesbury smacks (which used stow nets in the Wallet Channel), and bought sprat from them which they then hawked around Clacton.

Some lobstering continued at Walton, but beach boats faded out of use on the Tendring Hundred coast after World War II. At Clacton two young men, Mick Lynn and Steve Barrett, used to go out angling when they were at school and afterwards they did some part-time fishing when they worked. They believed that the Wallet (the channel off Clacton protected by the Gunfleet) and other Thames estuary sandbanks were rich fishing grounds, and in 1972 they took the plunge and became full time fishermen.

Mick Lynn says that their greatest asset was that fishing had died out and they could approach it with a completely open mind. Mick Lynn and Steve Barrett bought high speed fibreglass boats so that they could get out to their gear quickly. Mick Lynn's boat is a 14ft 'With 400' hull with a 30 hp outboard capable of 24 knots. In the mornings he can leave home at 5 a.m. and half an hour later be out in the Wallet working his gear. Speed is also important in unsettled weather, as they can get out and return before conditions deteriorate. The Wallet is slightly sheltered because on days when a 20ft northerly ground swell is breaking at Lowestoft and conventional beach boats cannot go off anywhere on the Suffolk coast, only a 5ft ground swell usually breaks on Clacton beach and these quite small craft can still go off.

This use of high speed craft has in a decade revived fishing off the Tendring Hundred beaches. Other young men have followed Lynn and Barrett so that in 1983 eight men worked from Clacton, one from Holland-on-Sea, two from Frinton and eight from Walton, although some of these worked from the Backwater, an inlet behind the town. These men mostly go in for ground nets to catch the fish that feed on the bottom. They go off about two hours before low water to haul their gill or trammel nets. Conventional longlines are used but when the sprat are in, they use trammel nets. The cod chase the sprat along the bottom and get caught in the trammel. There are times when the Wallet is absolutely dotted with plastic buoys and the danger in 1983 was that if too many more men took up fishing the stocks would be overworked. The pattern of expansion, boom and bust seems to affect many beach landings at different times.

One can travel the length of the Tendring Hundred coast by land or sea and never see a single beach boat except for some on the top of Frinton cliff. One bad effect of fishing dying out has been that the local council was totally hostile to the revival of fishing. All the boats have to be kept at their owners' homes and are trailed down to the beach every day.

At Clacton pleasure boats have worked off the beach and pier since Victorian times, but in recent decades the council has fought these pleasure boats tooth and nail. Dick Harman's *Nemo II* can be seen on any fine day in the Wallet running trips from Clacton, but although he has been operating boats here since 1960 he has had to fight the council the whole way.

Southend-on-Sea, at the mouth of the River Thames, had in Victorian and Edwardian times a large active fleet of pleasure boats catering for the masses from the East End of London who arrived by railway. This demand attracted Heywood from Deal to set up a boatbuilding yard on the Southchurch beach and in 1886 he launched the *Skylark* for the Lilly Brothers and the *Jubilee* in the following year for George and Alfred Myall. In 1888 the pleasure boats *May Queen* and *Storm King* were launched by Heywood, then the *Moss Rose* and *Four Brothers* and finally the largest of the sailing pleasure boats, the *Victoria* and the *Prince of Wales*. These pleasure boats were mostly gaff yawls, but had loose-footed mainsails like the Southend and Leigh fishing bawleys. In the winter the pleasure boats (or 'yachts' as they were advertised) went out 'stowboating' for sprat.

A gaff ketch taking on trippers for a shilling (5p) trip at Southend c.1935   (Hugh Perks)

80

Because of the sandbanks, boats could not use a drift net, but anchored and put a stow net down. In about 1880 Joe Myall's 40ft *Conqueror* was run down by a steamer while stowboating. Joe Myall successfully sued the owner of the steamship for the loss of his boat and had a new *Conqueror* built at Brightlingsea, but he failed to get 10 pence a bushel compensation for the sprat he claimed to have had in his hold.

The pleasure boats carried a good spread of canvas but when deeply loaded with passengers they were reputed to be 'as stiff as a church'. The larger boats ran trips for a shilling (5p) a head, over to Sheerness or the Nore lightship. The smaller boats were in fact fishing bawleys which just joined in pleasure boating at the height of the tripper season. There are tales of the bawleys sailing along, when the wind turned a bit cool, with the trippers all happily sitting on deck chairs down in the fish hold.

George Murrell bought an old Yarmouth beach yawl which he converted to a gaff ketch for pleasure work at Southend. She was advertised as 'Murrell's Lifeboat' which proved such a popular gimmick that Murrell had more boats built on the same lines.

Each family had its own 'pitch' on Southend's long seafront from which their boats sailed at high water. There was tremendous rivalry between the men on the East and West beaches, either side of the 1 mile long pier, famed for being the 'world's longest'.

In the nineteenth century the clinker double ended Norse hull gave way in most British local craft to decked carvel craft. The Leigh cockle boat *Mary Amelia* has few obvious features of her Norse ancestry. Here, in about 1919, she is loading hand raked cockles on a Thames Estuary sandbank. Similar methods of shell fishing were used in The Wash and Morecambe Bay   (Colin Fox)

As for the men from neighbouring Leigh creek, they were regarded as being hostile foreigners. When the Leigh men came to inspect or collect a new boat from Heywoods they came 'mob-handed' in a crowd in case (or perhaps in a hope) of a fight with the Southend men.

These were not true beach boats because they were never hauled out, but lay on moorings off the town. When the tide goes out over a mile off the foreshore the Southend flats are exposed. Getting off the beach and returning alongside the landing stages was a problem which was overcome by having long buoyed ropes laid off to an anchor.

The trippers also created a great demand for seafoods. The bawleys trawled for shrimps which were cooked on board and sold on landing. Sometimes in the late nineteenth century Southend and Leigh men started buying old Navy galleys (open pulling boats) from Sheerness and went down to the sandbanks after cockles. Later the sailing cockle boats were built as shallow versions of the bawleys. The last sailing boats built by Heywood were the sister ships *Reindeer* (now *Viking*) and the *Mary Amelia*, both 33ft and built in 1914 for Leigh owners. They were sailed down to the Maplin Sands on the Essex shore or to near the Columbine over by Whitstable. The cockle boats ran ashore at high tide and when the banks dried out the men gathered cockles, filled the boat and sailed home on the flood tide. To get there and back in a tide, they had to be fast.

Peters of Leigh also built cockle boats and seem to have taken on building pleasure boats when the Heywood yard closed. Peters built the sailing pleasure boat *Princess*, which like the *Coronation*, was about 27ft long and operated until the mid-1960s. The very last sailing pleasure boat at Southend was the 22ft gaff sloop *Irene*, built by Peters in 1957. With a crew of two she could carry thirty-five passengers, but with a single hand she only took twenty people. The *Irene* worked until 1971 and it is doubtful if any sailing pleasure boats were operated anywhere in Britain after her.

The last sailing barge owned at Southend was *Ashingdon* which was sold to become a houseboat in 1952. The sailing barges with their flat bottoms were ideal for working to beaches and creeks around the Thames Estuary, and Southend and the nearby village of Shoeburyness were regular beach ports. The trade to Southend was general goods to and from the town, but clay suitable for brick making was found in the Shoeburyness headland area. The Jubilee Brickfield at Thorpe Bay employed some barges, but the main trade was to the Shore Field and the Model Field on the edge of Maplin Sands at Shoeburyness. The oldest and largest of these fields was Shore Field started in about 1860 by J. Jackson.

At Shoeburyness, in a large shed at the end of Rampart Street, barges such as the *Shoebury* of 1879 and the *Scud* of 1898 were built. The barges *Curlew*, *Cheshire*, *Kestrel*, *Scud* and *Sigma* traded to Shore Field and also did some corn freights farther away. Eastwoods, the Kent brickmakers, were the last owners and seem to have closed the field after World War II. When sailing barges ceased to trade to Southend, yachts began to take their place. By 1983 the foreshore from Shoeburyness for four miles to Westcliff-on-Sea was dotted with yacht moorings.

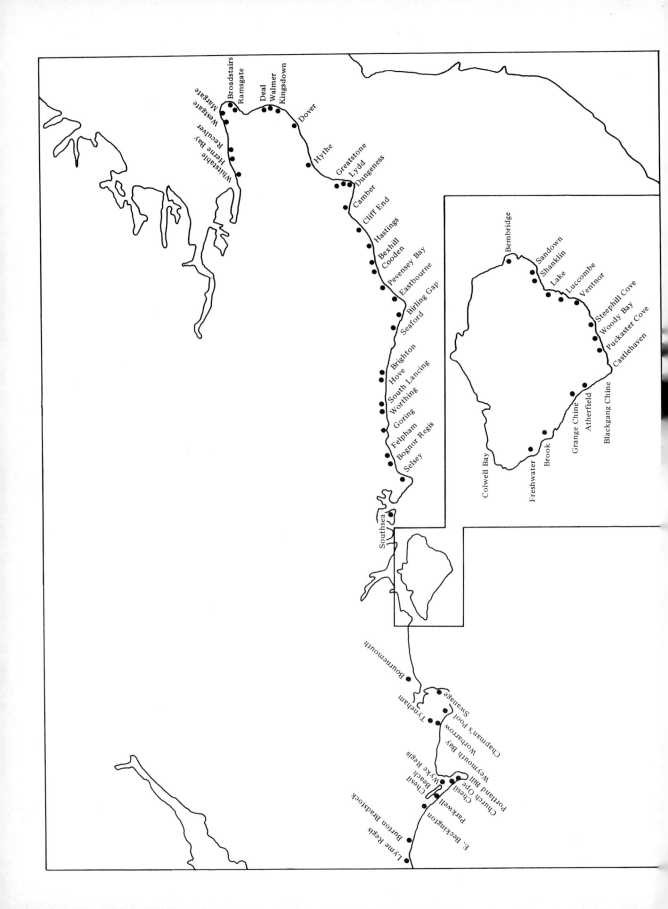

Chapter 5
Round the Foreland

Whenever one looks at the history of the coast of eastern Britain there is always the feeling that the Vikings are not far away. According to historical legend the Saxon migration into England started with the arrival in Kent of the Jute chief Hengest in 447. This landing is supposed to have taken place in Pegwell Bay on the east of the Isle of Thanet. Today in a little park, high above Pegwell Bay, sits the 71ft *Hugin*, a replica of a Viking longship which was rowed over from Denmark in 1949. The *Hugin*'s graceful hull shape must have been ideal for landing on beaches and certainly suggests that the Norse ship was the prototype of most British beach boats.

Apart from *Hugin*, there are few signs on the Kent coast now of the Viking age, but there is plenty of evidence of a later migration. This time it was Victorian holiday makers who descended on this coast because of its mild climate and sandy beaches. The forerunners of these invaders were brought from London in the hoys (sailing passenger craft) in the late eighteenth century. Then pleasure parties came by excursion steamers, after which the masses arrived by rail and now by car and coach.

The way people arrived greatly affected this coast. Today's car-borne visitors can spread out, but the rail travellers tended to stay within a short distance of the nearest railway station. This concentrated holiday-makers in quite small areas. In the days of rail, there were only a few shore amusements and people were much more inclined to go for trips on boats. At Whitstable, a couple of sailing boats were running trips off the beach to the east of the harbour during the summers of the Edwardian period. Earlier, to avoid harbour dues, sailing colliers had discharged on this beach into horse drawn carts.

In the nineteenth century a fleet of oyster smacks worked from Whitstable Horse Bridge, a slipway near the harbour entrance, but by 1982 the once famous Royal Whitstable Oyster warehouse and headquarters were closed and only a solitary smack, the *Gamecock*, lay on the traditional moorings off the beach.

Moving eastwards towards the North Foreland, there was a little beach boat activity at Herne Bay. A few angling boats are kept near the launching slipway but in 1982 one of the motor boats kept on moorings was attempting to revive full time whelking. The coast of Herne Bay is virtually straight and probably the term Bay was added to give holiday makers buying a railway ticket in Greater London the impression that they were going to the sandy cove of their dreams. However, Herne Bay was a beach landing long before tourism took over this coast because it was on the route to the Continent. In 1747 there was a passenger service by boat from London which landed on Herne beach. From here the passengers travelled across Kent by stage coach and then boarded another ship to take them across the English Channel. In 1832 there was a steamer service from London to the newly built pier at Herne Bay; from here a stage coach went to Dover. This traffic finished when the railway line was completed to the South Coast.

Before the railway reached Herne Bay there had been a regular trade in corn and coal from the beach, but afterwards only a few freights such as timber were discharged out of sailing barges in front of the Clock Tower. By the early 1900s 'trippers' were arriving by rail and to cater for them the clipper-bowed pleasure ketch *Duchess of York* ran trips from the beach out round the Girdlers lightship. East of Herne Bay the coast dips down to flat cattle and sheep grazing marshes. In the Saxon period this was a channel leading to Pegwell Bay, making Thanet an island. At the tip of the cliff-lined peninsula of the Isle of Thanet is the North Foreland, which marks the end of the North Sea. Thanet has sandy beaches and a low rainfall which attracted visitors to this area for at least two centuries. It is claimed that bathing machines were first invented at Margate, in the mid-eighteenth century. Today Thanet is thickly populated with the coastal towns of Margate, Broadstairs and Ramsgate almost joining up to form one urban area.

Thanet and neighbouring Herne Bay had its own type of beach boat. This was the Thanet wherry, a narrow pulling boat of about 18ft which was used for fishing and pleasure trips. The hull of the wherry was clinker, no doubt deriving from Norse traditions, but the hull shape was similar to the Deal galley and the Thames waterman's skiff, which suggests an eighteenth century origin. The term wherry is usually applied to passenger carrying craft. The Thanet wherry had a small transom stern so that the hull was virtually double-ended below the water. They were beached bows first; the fine stern parted the waves and prevented water from coming inboard.

There were two types of Thanet beach boats: the wherry, which had high sides, and the wherry-punt, which had low sides. Sometimes, if intended mainly for fishing, the wherry would be a little beamier. The hulls were usually varnished, a practice that was normal from Thanet right down to east Devon. The main builder of the Thanet wherries was Brockman at Margate, who turned them out in large numbers before World War I.

The Margate wherries were kept on the beach and when launched at low tide used a channel through the rocks to the east of the now demolished pier. To get the wherries into the water unique 'pole trucks' were used. These had two carriage wheels about 5ft high with a bar between them under which the boat was slung. The wherries were hauled out on the beach near the pier known as the Cold Harbour. The 50ft pleasure boats like the *Sunbeam* collected their passengers for trips off the end of the pier, but the wherries were hired from the beach. H. J. Parker recalled that as a boy of ten in about 1925, his father allowed him to hire out his *Mignonette*, a wherry built by Brockman in about 1890, in summer evenings. As well as hiring out boats, the Margate beachmen went out in the summer after lobsters in Kingsgate Bay. They used drift nets, known locally as beat nets, for herring, sprat and mackerel. When going out longer distances, a dipping lug sail was set, but unlike most beach boats they didn't carry ballast bags. During the short herring season some Margate men used the two-masted lug, 20–22ft, herring punts which were launched with pole trucks.

86

Between 1890–1939 there were about thirty boats working off Margate beach. At the start of World War II the British army was driven back to the French coast and the need to evacuate them quickly from Dunkirk beach caused an immediate round-up of all small craft in south eastern England. The Royal Navy sent a minesweeper to collect all the boats on Margate beach and the first ones lifted out of the water were actually smashed to bits in the process. Few of these boats ever returned to Margate from the Dunkirk evacuation. The Parkers traced their *Mignonette* to Chatham and had to pay for her to be returned by rail. On arrival it was found that the brass name plate, the pride of every Margate beachman, had been stolen from the stern.

At Broadstairs the wherries were kept on the beach in Viking Bay, under the shelter of the tiny pier. The sand is very fine, but sometimes a flint from the chalk cliffs found its way on to the beach and wherries were 'holed' coming ashore. The Broadstairs wherries were used for fishing and for hiring out. They were also used to put pilots onto vessels bound round the North Foreland in the Thames Estuary. The pilot wherries went 'seeking' vessels coming from the Downs. To try and combat the cold in the winter, some form of canvas cover was rigged, or even a fire on tiles was built in the bottom of the boat. Most men could just about stand the cold and wet in daylight, but at night the cold took the strength from the men and caused them to collapse. In Yorkshire the coblemen had the same problems when out drifting and they used to carry coal-burning braziers to keep them warm.

Vernon Kennard with the *Haughty Belle*, the last wherry at Margate, 1978   (Associated Kent Newspapers)

Deal boatmen in fine weather gear leaning on a capstan, 1886   (Paul Martin)

The last Thanet wherry being hired out was the *Joken* owned by Dusty Miller of Westgate. She was only about 12ft and being small was sometimes called a skiff. This vessel had been built by an apprentice of Brockman at Margate in 1939. In 1974 Vernon Kennard, who was starting to gather facts about this almost forgotten boat type, bought the *Joken*. Sadly, she was smashed to pieces on the beach at Kingsgate during a great storm in the following winter. Vernon Kennard then bought the *Haughty Belle* which had been built by Brockman in 1898 as the *Blossom*, and restored her, complete with rudder steered by yoke lines and with the rowlock holders on the outside of the hull. The *Haughty Belle* was taken out herring drifting until being sold to the National Maritime Museum in 1978. In 1982 the beaches of Thanet were empty of boats. Only at Broadstairs were there any signs of the traditional craft. In St George's Square there were four old wherries in a dilapidated state, while at the Bleak House Maritime Museum, a privately run venture, there was the wherry punt *Uncle George*, still with the high back seat in the stern for passengers, and the *Victoria*. All these craft were outside exposed to fresh water rain which breeds decay in wooden hulls.

At Ramsgate the beaches have been completely taken over by tourists, but there used to be wherries here as well. South of Ramsgate is Pegwell Bay, and then a sheltered area of water known as The Downs. It is protected from the prevailing south-west winds by high ground that stretches inland from the South Foreland. Five miles off the land are the notorious Goodwin Sands which run some nine miles up the Straits of Dover. The

Goodwins afford some protection to The Downs in an easterly breeze, but the anchorage can be very exposed in a north-easterly gale.

In the age of sailing ships The Downs were an important place of shelter for any ship bound through the Straits of Dover. This was not just British ships, but also those from the Northern European ports used to anchor here for shelter. In medieval times The Downs were a place where the King's ships assembled during the numerous wars with France. The Downs began to rise in importance during the Elizabethan era when English maritime interests were expanding. They were also used as a base for warships and for ships bound on ocean voyages; they called here to collect fresh food, mail and the final complement of passengers. The best place to land was the shingle beach at Deal and this town grew up largely to aid the service of passing ships. In fact no town in Britain owes its existence more to beach boats than Deal.

The Deal men were so important to England's maritime affairs that they were exempt from being pressed into the Royal Navy. Not only did Deal men attend the ships in The Downs, but they also acted as pilots. However, the short distance across to France made smuggling a very profitable business. In 1737 it was reported that about two hundred open boats were used for smuggling between the North and South Forelands. The most infamous attempt to suppress smuggling was in 1784 when it was suggested to the Prime Minister, Pitt, while he was staying at Walmer Castle that the Deal boats should be burnt. He waited until the boats were all hauled ashore in bad weather and then ordered

A Deal capstan was powerful enough to pull up a 40ft lugger by hand power   (Will Honey)

a regiment of soldiers to burn and smash all the boats while a naval cutter lay off-shore to prevent any from escaping.

This high-handed act seems to have only temporarily restrained the Deal men from smuggling. All through the Napoleonic War with France they carried on smuggling, but this even had its uses because the smugglers brought in news of events in France. With French ports only being about thirty miles away, The Downs were a front line naval base. Around four hundred men made a living off Deal beach, fetching and carrying from naval vessels. Nelson made several visits to The Downs in 1801 when he was in charge of defence craft between Orfordness and Beachy Head. He was very worried by the sight of West Indiamen sailing through The Downs, as these rich merchant ships would have made rich prizes for French privateers.

The importance of The Downs as a naval base reached a peak when in 1809 some seven hundred and fifty ships lay here to load troops for an invasion of Holland. The operation of taking out the soldiers was undertaken by about a hundred Deal luggers. The end of this war in 1814 saw a decline in men-of-war in The Downs which resulted in hard times amongst the Deal beachmen. However, the deep sea merchant ships continued to use The Downs, while the smaller coasters used the shallow waters of the Small Downs just to the north.

In fine weather the Deal men would take out pilots, dredge for lost anchors and supply ships with fresh food. But when the wind rose to gale force, the Deal men really came into their own. The windbound ships began labouring in the huge seas and started to drag their anchors. The Deal beachmen took out, at a price, spare anchors and chain. These anchors were those lost previously by other ships and then found by the beachmen by grappling. The anchors were stored in a field at the back of the town and then brought to the beaches on special carts so that they could be loaded on to the luggers as required.

The first aim of the Deal men was to save lives, but that alone could not 'feed a wife and family' and to make a living they had to save doomed ships and earn salvage money. Sailors viewed the Deal men with mixed feelings and often called them 'salvage sharks' because they preyed on other peoples misfortunes. Others who owed their lives to the timely arrival of a lugger when a ship was on the point of sinking said that the Deal men deserved every penny they earned. The truth lay somewhere in the middle, for the Deal men provided a much-needed service.

Because of the service they provided, the Deal luggers were famous all over the shipping world. Actually the luggers were not just owned in Deal, but also in the adjoining town of Walmer and the village of Kingsdown, just a little to the south. To the shipping world they were all Deal hovellers. The term hovelling was used to cover the combined services of pilots, salvagers and general runabouts in which the Deal men were so successfully engaged.

The beachmen clubbed together to operate a 'set' of boats. Each set had luggers, galleys, capstans and a gear store. The boat types were all evolved for a different purpose: the two-masted luggers were for going down the English Channel and putting pilots on incoming ships. These luggers were nearly 40ft long and were known as 'forepeakers' because of a small cabin forward of the foremast. The 'cat boats' were slightly smaller, but completely open. They were used for taking anchors and chain out to ships. Deal boats had oiled wood, with only the top plank outside being painted black.

The open boats included the 30–36ft galley punts which were sailed, but could be rowed, and the slightly smaller 27–32ft galleys which were rowed but could be sailed. The galleys are known to have existed in 1770 when they seem to have been chiefly involved in smuggling. The fast light galleys could be pulled across to France in about three hours and if spotted on the way back, one dodge was to land on the Goodwin Sands and drag the galley over and land in Kent before the Revenue Cutter could sail round. The galleys were also very good going through breakers and many ships' captains used to buy Deal-built galleys while lying in The Downs. However, galleys and luggers were sometimes lost and it is known that between 1860–87 fifty-three Deal men were drowned. Most lives were lost when running alongside and 'hooking on' to get a tow rope fast.

At Deal the ownership of the set of boats was often controlled by the landlords of the public houses. In bad weather the beachmen slept in the bar taprooms and passages, waiting for a call when a ship was in distress. The luggers were always launched bow first. Deal beach is very steep so the heavy luggers were able to gather enough speed while sliding down the greased skids to go right through the breakers and sail straight away from the beach. The galleys were launched stern first, but most of the Deal boats kept to a transom stern. Only a few adopted a 'beaching' or lute stern, as the south coast luggers did, which launched stern first.

Each lugger had its own 'stage' or place on the beach to which it had to be hauled back by large capstans. There were always enough old men and boys waiting on the beach to man the capstans, and everyone who helped were given a few pennies. When the Deal hovellers earned good money, the crews were too grand to lend a hand on the capstan, but when earnings sank, they had to join in this tedious task.

The clinker-built Deal luggers looked large when hauled up in lines on the beach, but they were really very small for the open sea. The forepeakers did have a tiny cuddy with bunks and a stove, but to live for over a week, especially during the winter months, in the open Channel in a half-decker was really tough. The cat boats were completely open with just a portable shelter known as a 'caboose' which was fitted between the thwarts. The galley punts were used just for carrying in The Downs, but the little galleys used to go away to sea for over a day, up into the Thames Estuary looking for ships to put pilots on. The galleys, under their square-cut lug sails, could be very wet at sea, and the men spent hours sitting in the driving spray.

Attempting to keep warm was a major part of the beachmen's lives. In wet conditions the men wore oilskins with trousers which reached up to their armpits, and long oilskin coats down to their knees. No buttons were used on these, only rope lashings. For top clothes the Deal men wore heavy pilot cloth jackets and trousers and leather wellington boots which were warmer than the modern rubber boots. The neck was protected by a long woollen scarf, often as long as four yards. In bad weather the great Victorian contribution to western civilization, the sou'wester, was worn, but in fine weather the Deal men proudly donned their sealskin caps.

The introduction of steam ships spelt the end of the Deal luggers. The steam ships did not have to wait for a fair wind and could proceed to their destination with only the occasional stop for bad weather. By the 1880s the Royal Navy no longer used The Downs on a regular basis; and steam tugs were picking up inward bound sailing ships at the end of ocean voyages and towing them straight through The Downs to the Thames. For as long as they lasted, some great square-rigged ships used The Downs in bad weather. One typical incident was in April, 1899, when the Aberdeen ship *Torridon*, the ship *Hesperides* and the barque *Port Sonachan* lay anchored about a mile off Deal beach in a blow. When the tide turned the *Torridon* lost an anchor while the crew were trying to shorten the anchor chain. This mishap was spotted from the watch towers on Deal beach and in a very short time a lugger was fastened on to the rigging of *Torridon* and five beachmen, all over sixty, were offering to sell a replacement anchor. The *Torridon*, however, had a spare anchor so that there was no need to buy another.

Although the coastal schooners and sailing barges sheltered in the Small Downs until World War II, there was not enough salvaging and hovelling to support the larger luggers after 1900. In 1909 the *Cosmopolite*, the last lugger left on Deal beach, was presented to the town council to be preserved as a memorial to the generation of beachmen who had served The Downs. The preservation of wooden vessels is a constant and skilful operation, but the *Cosmopolite* was just left sitting on Walmer beach exposed to wind and rain so she fell into disrepair and in 1925 was finally broken up.

Because they were cheaper to operate, the galleys and slightly larger galley punts went on being used in regular work until about 1919. The galleys were essentially a fast pulling boat, although they carried one lug sail, and for the summer regattas they set two

A pleasure boat loaded with trippers launching off Deal beach, c.1910   (Hugh Perks)

DEAL.

92

The Deal galley *Our Boys* after being refitted by Deal Rowing Club   (Will Honey)

lug sails. The galley punts or great galleys were also open boats, but were deep and could be used for carrying goods. By 1923 only six galleys remained on Deal beach, and these were kept by families to race in the Deal Regatta.

In 1952 only four galleys remained, the youngest being Thomas Upton's eight-oared *Seaman's Hope*, built of elm by Nichols of Deal in 1907, while the others probably dated from the early 1890s. In the mid 1950s galley racing was revived until one was smashed up coming ashore. After this *Saxon King* and *Undaunted* were lent to the Sea Scouts and they maintained and saved them. The *Saxon King* was eventually acquired by Deal Maritime and Local History Museum while in 1982 the *Undaunted* was still kept on Deal beach near the pier by Ben Bailey.

As we have seen, hovelling declined at Deal from around 1880 and after this the beachmen changed over to fishing instead. In this they were in direct conflict with the tradesmen and hotel owners who wished to develop Deal as a summer resort. For fishing the Deal men used fore-mizzen punts, open luggers of about 15ft in length, which were used for drift netting for sprat, herring and mackerel.

In the summer some beach men fitted out their luggers with gaff sails as pleasure boats. They were launched, with their sails set, off steep beaches in the usual manner, which must have been quite an experience for the passengers who sat packed tightly on their seats. The steep beach and the weight of the craft gave the Deal luggers enough speed to go right through the breakers and sail straight away from the beach.

The galley *Our Boys* beaching at
Deal, c.1948   (Will Honey)

To the town councillors, pleasure boats were welcome on the beach, but boats for
fishing and hovelling were not because their activities were not what the visitors wanted.
Matters were made worse by an abnormal high tide in 1897 which eroded away much
of North End beach so there was nowhere for the large luggers to land. Some of the
luggers engaged in fishing moved to Walmer and Kingsdown instead.

In spite of an extension to the Parade in 1911, the South End at Deal remained a
beach landing, although even this has now been eroded away. Today the beach boats sit
perilously perched on a narrow strip of shingle between the sea and the Parade. In 1971
I watched C. Hickman & Son's *If Not* coming ashore on the South End and she looked
to me to have some of the qualities of the sailing lugger. The clinker hull was much
deeper than an ordinary motor launch, just as the old luggers and galley punts had been
very deep. However, the wooden Deal boats built after World War II often had painted
hulls, although some followed the old tradition of showing the wood grain by

94

varnishing. Deal motor boats are launched stern first because with a reverse gear they can easily pull away from the beach.

In 1971 the Deal fishermen told me that they could not make a living by just fishing and they relied on taking out summer angling parties to help with their costs. The wrecks around the Goodwins prove particularly good grounds for rod and line fishing. I was told of the day when three hundred angling boats were anchored around the Goodwins. Coaches brought parties from as far away as London for a day's fishing. Deal is reputed to attract more anglers than any other place in Britain.

In the winter fishermen go long lining for cod and skate, each line having a thousand hooks baited with sprat, and they also do some herring drifting. Fish is sold on the beach or to one of the fish shops in Deal. If there is a sudden flush of fish then fishermen club together for a lorry to take them to a larger market. Once Deal had its own fish cannery. This started in 1892 and was supplied by about thirty luggers working from Deal, Walmer and Kingsdown and another group working from Dungeness. The whole enterprise is said to have given employment to about three hundred people. This was followed by a fish paste factory which finally closed in the 1930s because local fish stocks declined.

Supplying and repairing craft for the beachmen of Kent once kept several small boatyards active. However, as the fishing declined and wood became progressively more expensive, this also declined. It seems that the last wooden boat built at Deal was the *Golden Vanity* built by Bob Abel in about 1974.

In 1981 about a hundred and fifty men and one woman were licenced to take out boats from Deal. On Deal beach there were 114 numbered spaces and 123 on Walmer beach. Most of the beach boats were for angling, but the Deal & Walmer Inshore Fishermen's Association still had fourteen members at Deal and eight at Walmer who were full-time fishermen so that the strong traditions of working beach boats lives on.

Just south of Walmer is the little village of Kingsdown, which was once a beach landing. Kingsdown men did some hovelling but were mainly concerned with fishing. In the October 1865 mackerel season, the Kingsdown men landed £1000 worth of fish in ten days. This represented about £30 per man which was 'big money' for the period. Fishermen have invariably earned a lot of money in short spaces of time, followed by long periods without earning anything. It is difficult to transfer 1860 values into modern terms. However, the Kingsdown fishing lugger *Pilgrim* was built at Deal in 1872 for £400. At that time mackerel fishing was paying well, with Deal, Walmer and Kingsdown luggers reported coming ashore 'dangerously laden' and the crews sharing out £80–£100 for a night's work.

Another Kingsdown boat was the 38ft forepeaker *Lady Rosa*, built at Deal in 1874 and winner of the first class luggers race in 1884 Deal Regatta. This period was the height of Kingsdown as a fishing station, because by 1905 there appeared to be only the luggers *Anne* and *Louisa* left here. By the time James Birch, master of the *Louisa*, died in 1920, all the luggers had gone from Kingsdown. When I visited the village in 1981 there was no sign that it had ever been a beach landing, just waves breaking lazily on the empty shingle beach.

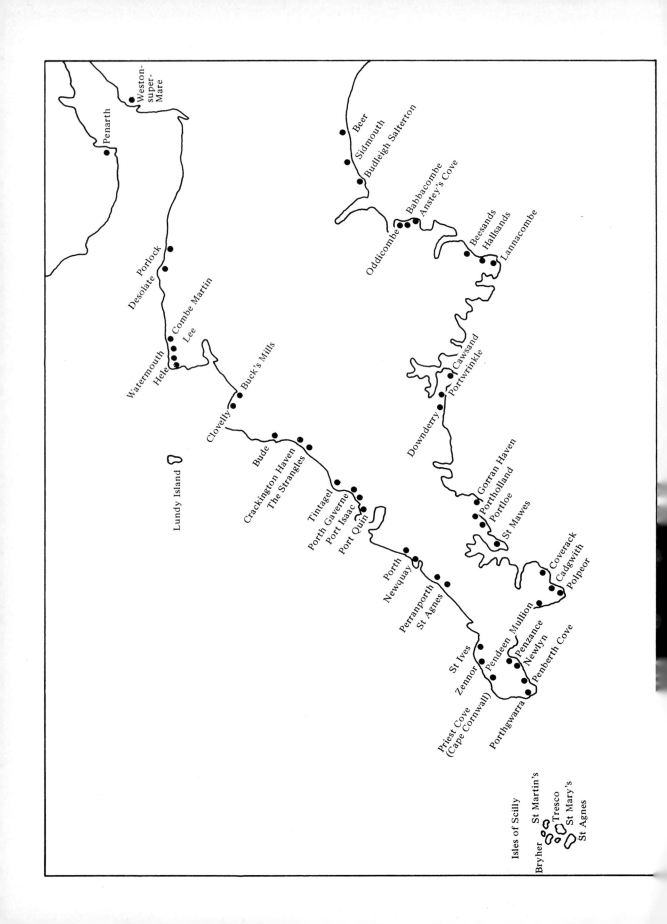

Weston-
super-
Mare

Penarth

Beer

Sidmouth

Budleigh Salterton

Babbacombe

Anstey's Cove

Beesands

Hallsands

Lannacombe

Oddicombe

Porlock

Desolate

Combe Martin

Lee

Watermouth

Hele

Buck's Mills

Cawsand

Portwrinkle

Clovelly

Downderry

Bude

Crackington Haven

The Strangles

Gorran Haven

Portholland

Portloe

St Mawes

Tintagel

Port Gaverne

Port Isaac

Port Quin

Coverack

Cadgwith

Polpeor

Porth

Newquay

Perranporth

St Agnes

Pendeen Mullion

Penzance

Newlyn

Penberth Cove

Porthgwarra

St Ives

Zennor

Priest Cove
(Cape Cornwall)

Lundy Island

Isles of Scilly

St Martin's

Tresco

St Mary's

St Agnes

Bryher

Chapter 6
Down Channel

Over the centuries the beaches of southern England have seen plenty of activity by smugglers. The sheer problem of watching every possible landing place loaded the odds heavily in favour of the smugglers. This 'free trade' got off to a real start in 1296 when the government of the day attempted to keep down the price of wool at home by putting a tax on all wool exported to the continent. For several centuries the government tried to prevent goods leaving the country, but then in the eighteenth century the tide turned the other way. The government placed an import duty on luxury goods such as tea, spirits, silk and tobacco. In theory, all these goods should have been landed on a legal quay and payment made at the local customs house. In fact, vast quantities were landed on open beaches and were eagerly bought by the gentry and common people alike.

The government appointed Customs officers to cover the whole coast, but they were openly flouted by the smugglers. To give the Customs and Excise officers more authority, the Smugglers Act of 1736 brought in tougher sentences such as the death penalty for wounding or hindering a Customs Officer, while if caught giving night signals within six miles of the coast the sentence was transportation. The Act also authorized the payment and free pardons to informers, but this hard line approach merely signalled the start of open war between smugglers and customs officers.

Smuggling by ruthless and highly organized gangs became common all over Britain, but between Kent and Cornwall it was a major industry involving almost the whole coastal community. Many people saw little harm in the 'free trade'. The eighteenth century authoress Elizabeth Carter deplored the sight of carriages of 'people of first rank in the land leaving Deal laden with every kind of contraband'.

By the late eighteenth century smuggling gangs were so heavily armed that to try and seize goods, the Customs Officers had to be backed up by a detachment of Dragoons. In 1780 a Customs Officer and Dragoons seized 183 tubs of Geneva gin from smugglers at Whitstable. The Dragoons were taking this to Canterbury when a gang of fifty smugglers attacked them on the open road and shot a Dragoon before recovering the gin. A reward of £50 was offered and later one of the smugglers was caught and hanged on Penendon Heath.

The Hawkhurst gang of Rye were the most notorious of the eighteenth century smugglers. They used to drink in the Mermaid Inn at Rye, sitting with cutlasses and pistols lying on the tables in front of them. Drawn by thoughts of reward, two men set off to Chichester to lay information against the gang. They stopped for a drink on the way and unwisely told of their plans. This was quickly passed on to the Hawkhurst gang who overtook the men, tortured them in a grotesque way and buried one alive and threw the other down a well and stoned him to death. These two murders lead to a detachment of Dragoons going to Rye, and after a fight the Hawkhurst gang was rounded up and later twenty were hung and left hanging in chains as a warning to others.

During the Napoleonic War, smuggling continued unchecked and the fact that Britain was at war with France only made it more profitable. Once the fighting stopped, Britain turned part of its naval force into a coastal blockade which lasted from 1818 to 1831. In 1820 a gang operating from Herne Bay were involved in a series of fights before being overpowered by the Prevention Service.

One of the last strongholds of the smuggling gangs was Romney Marsh. Here there were not only plenty of lonely beaches, but only local men knew the tracks through the marsh. In 1821 there was the notorious Battle of Brookland near Rye, in which the Aldington gang was captured by the Coastal Blockade. Another battle was fought in the Sussex Inn and New Inn in 1828 at Sidley Green near Bexhill, when two smugglers were killed. In all, eight smugglers of the Sidley gang were sentenced to death, but later this was altered to transportation to a convict settlement in New South Wales.

The tide really turned against the smugglers in 1822 when the new HM Coastguard service was started. It was several years before this was properly established, but eventually the whole coastline was covered by the ever-watchful eyes of the Coastguards. The Coastguards built and rented houses near every possible beach landing and became part of the community, so that they could pick up information to make smuggling impracticable.

Smuggling certainly did not stop just because there were neat coastguard cottages all round the coast, but the presence of such a body of men did curtail it. Since World War II the emphasis of the coastguard service has switched much more on to co-ordinating rescue services. In this period the beaches of Kent and Sussex have, because of being a 'stepping stone' between London and the Continent, once more been the scene of another smuggling era. In 1967 I was in Ramsgate on the Baltic ketch *Solvig* when a fast motor cruiser came alongside. The owners happily showed us over and were very proud of their high powered ship-to-shore radio, then quite rare in pleasure craft. They explained that it was essential for 'angling parties' which paid 'very well'. Later, when we heard the motor cruiser was being sort by police in connection with the landing of illegal Asian immigrants, we fully understood the reason for their radio. Dungeness is reputed to have been the place where many of Britain's new citizens first stepped ashore. However, in about 1971, Essex fishermen were being offered £500 a head to smuggle in Pakistanis. At about this time late-night anglers on Shingle Street beach in Suffolk were very surprised to see a party of Asians walking past carrying suitcases. The running of illegal immigrants in the early 1970s was briefly a revived use for the beaches in southern and eastern England, as used by smugglers. The introduction of four wheel drive Land Rovers made this easier because they could drive right down on to the beach to pick up their passengers.

Fishing is now the main occupation of beach boats of south-east Kent. In 1983 four boats were working off the beach at Hythe and another eight boats ran angling trips.

It was probably smuggling which first drew people to go and settle on Dungeness, that great flat shingle headland jutting into the English Channel. Today, on the eastern sheltered side of Dungeness, there are about a hundred boats dotted along the beach for about five miles. The first group is at Greatstone, but the oldest landing here appears to be Lade, which in the early 1920s had nine boats. Because of the shallow water here boats can only be launched and landed for about four hours on every tide. This did not matter in the days of sail, because the boats used to run ashore at low water and horses and carts came across the flats from Greatstone and collected the catch.

The hamlet of Lade was then just a few 'black houses' (the fishermen tarred everything) and two pubs, the Ship and the Jolly Fishermen. There were no roads to Lade and everyone travelling on Dungeness had to walk across several miles of shingle, while goods arrived on special wide wheeled beach carts. About 1930 a road was built to a lighthouse on the end of Dungeness and within a few years this was lined with holiday bungalows. The road at Lade originally ran beside the sea, but the beach has receded. A hand capstan which Harry Young put beside the new road has had to be continually moved so that in 1983 it was a hundred yards east of the road. The capstan is still maintained, looking with its huts for all the world like a nineteenth century print, but a motor winch is used to haul up the part-time fishing boats *Mermaid* and *Iona*.

The *Iona* and *Mermaid* at Lade, Dungeness, 1983. Note the railway truck on the left   (Author)

The road does not run near to the point where the larger craft are landed on the sheltered south east side of Dungeness. To get bulk catches like sprat to the road, fishermen built railway lines to link the beach to the road. Each group of boats had a railway and truck, but now a hard track has been developed so that fishermen can get their cars down to the beach. In 1983 thirteen decked trawlers worked off Dungeness beach, mostly decked clinker wooden hulls of the traditional South Coast type. The Dungeness and Hastings boats have in recent decades been built of elm on oak by H. L. Phillips & Son at their yard on the Rock Channel, Rye. In 1983 Derek Phillips told me that, due to the recession, they had not built any for about a year.

In the summer the population of Rye is outnumbered by the people at the huge holiday camp at Camber. It was on these sands that the Battle of Brookland started in 1821 when about 250 smugglers of 'The Blues' or Aldington Gang were surprised by men from the Coastal Blockade. Most of the fighting, in which four smugglers were killed, sixteen seriously wounded and one midshipman died, actually took place inland as the gang took the cargo away. By 1900 Camber was used for kettle net fishing, that is, nets hung between poles; at low tide the mackerel were shovelled into horse carts. The opposite side of Rye Bay, sheltered by the high ground at Fairlight, is Cliff End where several boats are kept, but the main beach landing of this section of the coast is at Hastings.

Bob Tart and his father fitting up a trawl on Dungeness beach, 1966   (Fishing News)

The beach used by the fishermen at Old Hastings is known as the Stade. This name came from the Old English word meaning a landing place. However although Hastings is one of the oldest fishing ports in the British Isles, the actual beach has only been used since the Elizabethan period. In the medieval period before this, Hastings was one of the privileged Cinque Ports and there was actually a small creek harbour here. This creek was closed by silt deposited across the mouth by the eastern drift of the tide and is now buried under the present site of the Memorial and Cricket Ground. In spite of the creek being closed, Hastings remained an important fishing centre.

From the Elizabethan period to the nineteenth century Hastings was a beach port. The ships had to wait for the right conditions to land. For instance, in January 1850, ten colliers arrived off Hastings only to have to scurry back to The Downs for shelter because of a stiff south-west wind. The Hastings built *Lamburn* traded regularly for thirty-three years, but was finally wrecked on her 'home port' in 1866. The brig *Pelican*, also Hastings built, traded here for forty-one years. On a wild November night in 1879 she was being hauled off the beach when the rope broke. The *Pelican* was thrown broadside on to the beach and stayed there being hammered by the waves all night. When the wind dropped the ballast was taken out of *Pelican* and she was hauled off and taken into Rye where it was found that she was too badly damaged to repair. She was the last Hastings trader; the arrival of the railway killed the need for cargoes to be unloaded on The Stade.

Fishing from Hastings seems to have been very successful in the early nineteenth century. Most fish were sold locally, but some were taken by horse and van to Billingsgate. In order to get the fish to London fresh, the horses were kept at a gallop and a fresh team took over every ten miles. After the Napoleonic War ended in 1815 Hastings boats used to go into French ports to sell their catch. The French government later imposed duties to stop this, but Hastings men then sold to French boats they met at sea. If the French skipper did not have enough money to pay them, the lugger's boy was left with the Hastings skipper as security.

The Hastings fishermen had by the early nineteenth century adopted the three-masted lugger, which according to many nautical reference books were copied from the French rig. However it is not as simple as that, because many French historians state that the lugger originated in the English smuggling craft and was first adopted by the French Navy before the American Revolution in 1776. In 1772 a young French naval officer appears to have been in England 'surreptitiously taking off' the underwater lines of a lugger. The truth about the origins of the fast sailing luggers was that they developed as a result of a cross-pollination of ideas from both sides of the English Channel.

In the mid-nineteenth century the main Hastings fleet was engaged in drift net fishing, but little of their time was spent in home waters. From January to July the boats were down in the west country after mackerel, and from September to December they were in the North Sea after herring. Because they were not landing on the beach daily, the Hastings boats were, at this stage, able to have fine lines and were fast, 50ft three-masted luggers. They were very similar to the Yarmouth luggers and both were noted for their speed, a characteristic which had lasted from the old smuggling days.

The Hastings lugger's reputation for speed lead to Lord Willoughby De Eresby ordering a lugger for shooting and fishing in 1855, from Frederick Tutt & Son of

Eastwell, Hastings. The result was the 34 ton *Leopard* which proved an able seaboat, and De Eresby went on and ordered the 100 ton *Panther* from Tutt. Following her, De Eresby had Tutt build the huge 134ft, 220 ton 3 masted lugger *New Moon* in 1859. This yacht must have been one of the largest craft ever built at a British beach landing and certainly one of the fastest, as she could make up to 13 knots.

The famous net shops on Hastings beach are a link with the three masted luggers because originally a net shop was built for each lugger with the wood left over from the new hull. Each shop had a base only 8ft square, yet some rise 30ft high and have three storeys and even in some cases a cellar for storing fish. The term net shop is like a workshop, in fact a place where the nets were repaired. The height dates back to the time when space was short on the beach and ground rent was high. Another advantage of the net shops was that twice a year, between voyages, the luggers were hauled up by horse capstan between the shops. A plank was put across from the second floor and nets and other gear carried across to the luggers at deck level. In 1846 and again in 1961 many of the tarred wooden net shops were destroyed by fire, but each time the public raised the money to have them rebuilt. In 1957 some of the more decayed shops were pulled down, but forty-three were repaired. Since the beach has continued to extend, fishermen have built flat-roofed huts lower down, but the net shops are still in regular use and can only be used by working fishermen.

In the mid-Victorian period, Hastings was losing its position as a leading fishing port as Yarmouth, Lowestoft and the west country ports increased their own drift net fleets. No one is certain when the three-masted luggers finished at Hastings, but they appear to have gone by about 1870. Instead, the Hastings men concentrated on trawling in Rye Bay and around the Channel banks. Since the boats were away just one tide (as they still are) there was a switch to smaller 30ft two-masted luggers known as 'trawl boats'. Speed was no longer of so much importance, but survival through the breakers was, so that the hulls were built beamy and they had bluff bows to give plenty of buoyancy. The inspiration for this type of hull may have come from the Dutch 'Bomshuits' seen in the North Sea or from the French coast, because there is a strong resemblance with the beach boats used around Boulogne. This coast was originally part of Dutch-speaking Flanders and even in the nineteenth century the links with The Netherlands were still strong.

The Hastings trawl boats were periodically swamped coming ashore in bad weather. The practice was for a man to wade out in the surf with an axe and smash open the hull low down near the stern. This let the water escape and released the weight so that the boat could be dragged up the beach to safety. To minimize the danger, as they were launched stern first, the lute stern was introduced in about 1880. This is an extension of the hull which curves out so that the breaking waves tend to lift the stern. The lute stern became standard practice all along the Sussex coast and in about 1900 there was a progression of this idea with the short counter or 'elliptical' stern. However, the Hastings men kept to the clinker hull. In about 1887 some of the small trawl boats and

The *Mayflower* and *Breadwinner* and their carts at Hastings just after World War II. After Will Curtis' lugger *EVG* was blown up by a mine in 1943, he had the auxiliary lugger *Breadwinner* built in a barn at Pevensey. Because of war time shortages the wheelhouse was made from four doors. The punt astern of *Breadwinner* belonged to Jim Curtis   (Author's Collection)

open punts were given centreboards to improve their ability to sail against the wind, however these boards were a constant trouble because of stones jamming.

In 1897 there was an attempt to build a harbour at Hastings. This failed, but part of the west harbour arm was built and this still proves useful shelter for the landing. In 1912 the first engine, a 13 hp Kelvin, was fitted to a Hastings boat. This was bitterly opposed by the older generation, but over the next decade most trawl boats, small 'bogs' and open punts were fitted with an engine. Just after World War I auxiliary sailers were built complete with mizzen, dipping forelug and jib set on a 'jib boom' (bowsprit), but they had small engines when built. The depression of the early 1920s stopped the whole fleet from being replaced. The sailing trawlers were fitted with engines and kept on working until they wore out. The last of the First Class trawl boats, over 15 tons, was the *E.V.G.* which was blown up by a mine in World War II.

After World War II the *Industry*, built in 1870, and the oldest boat on the beach, was presented to the Hastings Corporation for preservation. The *Industry*'s claim to fame was that she had been to the Dunkirk Evacuation in 1940. However the town had little will to save this old timer and instead she was burnt as a bonfire on November 5. Her tar soaked hull gave the crowd brief entertainment, which has been the fate of a great many beach boats. The *Enterprise*, a trawling lugger built at Hastings in 1912, escaped the November 5 solution. In 1956 the Fishermen's Church was converted to a museum and after removing the south wall the *Enterprise* was placed inside.

After World War II the Hastings fishermen, with the help of White Fish Authority grants, updated their fleet. The last man building decked boats on Hastings beach was Alfred Philcox, who, in the late 1940s, built a series of craft which the government sent out to Nigeria. From the timber left over Philcox built the 30ft *Wendy Mary* in 1951, which was rigged out with a traditional lug rig and sailed for pleasure. Most of the decked craft were built at Rye and a few at Whitstable. These are called simply 'Big Boats' to distinguish them from the smaller and newer open 'punts'. The 'Big Boats' were originally trawlers, but many have now switched to the more successful trammel nets like the punts.

One reminder of the age of sail is the 28ft decked *Edward & Mary* which was built on Hastings beach in 1919 as an auxiliary sailer. She had lug sails and a 13 hp Kelvin petrol/paraffin engine and was engaged in trawling, drifting and some long lining, but the latter method was soon abandoned at Hastings. Most of the Hastings boats carried sails until the diesels were introduced in the 1950s. About then *Edward & Mary* was sold to Eastbourne, where most of the fishing is done fairly well inshore on the banks off towards the Royal Sovereign lightvessel. She was used mainly for trawling until 1982, and the following year was sold to Steve Peak to be restored at Hastings.

The Hastings men have tried to keep to decked craft because of the dangers when beaching on this exposed coast. In busy times around a dozen boats a month, particularly open ones, have problems on launching and landing. Sometimes it is just a matter of a couple of days work to sort out a flooded engine, but occasionally it is more serious, such as the time just before Christmas in 1981 when Fred White's *Nicola Dawn* filled in the surf. Unfortunately the engine kept running and bent the pistons and rods so that the engine had to be totally rebuilt. Bill Easter, skipper of the 18ft *Sea Star*, told *Fishing News* that launching off an open beach can never be taken for granted, the knack being to wait for a smooth wave and then catch it. But he said 'Bet your life a big wave will follow and you'll be filled in'.

In spite of the obvious dangers of working off Hastings beach, it has the largest fleet of any British beach landing. In 1982 there were forty-six boats ranging from 18ft to 33ft working from Hastings, nearly a quarter of the full time boats on the Sussex fishing register. With the laid-up craft and angling boats to the west of the harbour arm there were about a hundred and fifty boats on Hastings beach. With the net shops, fish market and the boats (which were even more picturesque in the days of sail), the beach here has attracted visitors for over a century. But at many south coast resorts the tourist industry drove, in one way or another, the fishing boats off the beach.

The first practical reason for the Hastings fleet's continued existence is that the local fishing grounds remain productive and can be reached in 'one tide', but more important, the fishermen actually own the lower beach. A charter by Queen Elizabeth I gave the fishermen the right to land free on this beach. The fishing community has remained united to protect its interests for a long time. The first fishermen's association was started in about 1832 and this in turn led to the creation of the Fishermen's Institute &

The Hastings fleet shore bound in bad weather, 1966. They were nearly all Big Boats at this time. In the foreground are the Fish Market and Netshops   (Fishing News)

The lute sterned RX27 starting to be hauled up at Hastings, 1983   (Author)

Association in 1882. Fishing and tourism both need sheltered beaches, so there are bound to be conflicts of interest.

Sussex has high concentration of beach boats, but while the beach at Old Hastings has grown larger since the building of the breakwater in about 1839, the one at Bulverhythe at the western end of the huge Hastings–St Leonards tripper seafront, is being steadily eroded away. The open punts at Bulverhythe have an uncertain future. The same is true of Cooden, the shingle landing at the west end of Bexhill, which also suffers from erosion. At Cooden only the punts *Breadwinner*, *Mona Lisa* and *Tricia* remain while further west at Pevensey Bay over one hundred boats remain. About half a dozen worked from the centre of Pevensey Bay beach with trammel, gill and trawl nets. The beach is sheltered by Langney Head and it was on this beach in 1833 that the Battle of Pevensey Sluice took place, which was the last running fight between old-style smugglers and the prevention service.

Eastbourne is sheltered by the 534ft high Beachy Head and about sixty boats are kept here. Only ten are full-time fishing craft and most are traditional Sussex craft with the elliptical stern built by Lower at Newhaven, but the Eastbourne-built *Horizon N* is a new approach to beach boats. She is a steel sterned trawler, about 28ft long, 10ft beam, almost flat bottom and has two propellers in raised chambers under the stern. These craft are kept to the east of the town, but the original 'fishing station' was on the beach in the middle of the town.

Eastbourne, like so much of southern England, has a mild climate, and in the Victorian period it developed as a resort and residential town. Fishing boats on the sea front did not fit in with the genteel image that the town's developers wished to create. In the 1880s the town council ordered the fishermen to move off the beach so that the Royal Parade could be constructed. The fishermen refused to move and hauled an old lugger across the rails of the contractor's light railway, but it was smashed up by the engine. Reluctantly the fishermen were forced to move to the eastern end of the beach.

The Victorian Eastbourne luggers were very similar to the Hastings boats but had finer lines and were faster. The 'Bourners' went after herring to Southern Ireland and on mackerel voyages to Yorkshire. Although their boats were called luggers, some were fitted with gaff mainsails. They only returned to Eastbourne between voyages to change their nets. As the luggers were up to 40ft long, they had to be hauled up the beach with a steam capstan, but there were smaller 28ft long two-masted luggers known as 'Shinamen' which were half decked and worked off the beach daily. The increasing number of hotels provided a ready market for the lobsters landed.

A pleasure boat and rowing skiff for hire on Brighton beach in about 1902 with the fishing fleet anchored off shore. The large pleasure boat owned by Fred Collins in the centre was taking on passengers ready to slide down into the water   (Brighton Library)

Of the gentlemen who visited Eastbourne, one of them, F. W. Leybourne Popham, a Wiltshire landowner, became absolutely fascinated with the luggers. He commissioned the Eastbourne builder George Gausden to build the 70ft auxiliary steam lugger *Paradox* in 1888 which did some racing in the Solent. Popham became obsessed by the belief that the dipping luggers could beat the great gaff schooner yachts. He commissioned the famous yacht designer William Fife to design the schooner lugger *White Slave* which was built by Gausden of Eastbourne in 1890. The *White Slave* was very fast, but the dipping lug sail, which was perfectly satisfactory for fishermen who went off the beach on one tack and came back on another, was too cumbersome for racing round buoys.

As well as yachts, Popham built up a fleet of fishing luggers and brought in Lowestoft men to get full crews. He had two steam carriers *Romulus* and *Remus* to bring the fish back when his five luggers were working out of Irish ports. In about 1892 Popham started to lose interest in his Eastbourne ventures (it is quite possible that it was losing him money) and he moved his boating interests to Hythe on Southampton Water.

West of Beachy Head are the chalk cliffs known as Seven Sisters and the Birling Gap landing is below a dip in these cliffs. This is an extremely awkward place to keep a boat because they have to be dropped down a sheer cliff of about 30ft to a boulder beach. The Birling Gap Safety Boat Association keep their craft in a shed near the sheer edge of the cliff. However the rocks off the coast form good lobster grounds and make it worthwhile for the Bognor GRP boat *Sharlisa* to be worked part time from the cliff.

A lute sterned beach boat running trips off Bexhill beach, c.1905. The Sussex lugger set a jib on a bowsprit   (Author's Collection)

There have long been a small number of boats potting from Seaford, but the beach here is near the entrance to Newhaven harbour and most of the local fishing fleet is based there. Until the late nineteenth century most of the fish landed in Sussex and south Kent came from beach boats. Hastings, Eastbourne, Brighton and Worthing were the major fishing centres, but the creation of better harbours at Dover, Folkestone, Newhaven and Shoreham undermined the importance of the long-established beach landings.

West of Newhaven, the coast for about thirty miles is virtually built up all the way to Selsey Bill. The high residential population and the visitors from London have resulted in hundreds of open boats being kept on the beaches for angling and part-time fishing. Because the summer visitors are of such commercial importance to the coast, the beach landings here are very orderly. Each boat is allowed to have only a low chest in which the winch and gear are stored.

It is difficult now to think of Brighton as being a major fishing centre, but it was until the end of the nineteenth century. Brighton's rise as a resort started in the mid-eighteenth century when a Sussex doctor Richard Russell, proclaimed that sea bathing and sea air were major health cures. Being near to London, Brighton gradually attracted the rich and fashionable people, but its real leap to fame came in 1783 when the Prince of Wales came for a visit. He was very impressed with Brighton and set about turning it into the mecca for the Regency gentry. Brighton was already a well established fishing centre; in 1580 there had been eighty boats and in 1793 the town had forty-five mackerel fishing boats and another twenty-five trawling boats.

The Brighton boats were called 'hog boats' or 'hoggies' and were about 28ft long, with an incredible 16ft beam which was virtually half their length. They were rigged with two spritsails and were slow sailors, but rode the seas like contented ducks. The true 'hoggie' dropped from favour in the 1880s and they were replaced with luggers similar to the Hastings boats. The fish market on the beach led to the Cornish drifters and Lowestoft trawlers landing here. Then the Brighton men started buying Cornish boats and often worked out of Shoreham, but John Plugh continued building at Brighton and his last lugger, the *Elizabeth II*, was launched in 1910. There were two sailing luggers, the *Belinda* and the *Victory*, left on the beach when World War II started, but the Admiralty ordered that these should be broken up so that they would not be in the way if an invasion had to be fought off.

When I first visited Brighton in 1953 there were still elliptical sterned boats working off the beach just east of the Palace Pier. Now most of the open boats are kept in orderly lines behind the fun fair.

The massive holiday activities dominate the seafront at Brighton and Hove, but in 1860 the First Avenue Boat Station at Hove was run by Mr Voysey. The surname is French Huguenot. In the seventeenth century these French Protestant fishermen came and settled on the South Coast to escape persecution by the Roman Catholic church. Many surnames in the Dungeness area, such as Tart, are also Huguenot. The fishing at Hove and Brighton gave way to pleasure boating early in this century.

Numerically British beach boats must have been at their peak in the 1890s, because most traditional beach fishing fleets were then at their height. There were also numbers of tripper boats and skiffs for hire on the beaches of every resort. Many new resorts such

The pleasure boat *Skylark* passing what appears to be Brighton West Pier in about 1895. In the pleasure boats working off the beach the lug sail was replaced with the gaff sail because it was much easier to handle when turning to windward   (Graham Jensen)

as Southsea, Swanage, Cleethorpes, Penarth, Llandudno, Dovercourt and The Reculver had tripper boats. The tripper boats of Brighton landed to the west of the Palace Pier; they were referred to as yachts and had counter sterns and gaff sails, but the same beamy hulls as the Sussex beach fishing boats. The tripper boats operated by Fred Collins were loaded with passengers, had their sails set on the beach, and were then pushed off by long poles. These pleasure yachts were pulled back ashore by large horse-operated wooden capstans.

Worthing no longer has any large decked craft, but there are many lute sterned open boats here, at South Lancing and Goring. Many beachmen call this a 'counter' and seldom differentiate between the three types of South Coast stern. The landings at Worthing are very neat, but in 1983 there were still four wooden bar capstans on the beach. The sea off Worthing is shallow and kettle nets used to be used on the sands between Worthing and South Lancing.

Worthing fishermen believe that the wooden lute stern Sussex boats are better for landing because they are heavy and carry way through the surf, while the lighter GRP Condor Bognor boats tend to be thrown sideways. However in bad weather, on this long flat beach, there is always the danger for a boat of any type. The owner of the *Faithful Kitty*, a GRP Condor boat made in 1981, said that when coming in in a Force 7 loaded with nets he had been swamped. On another similar occasion a wooden Sussex

110

boat was also swamped and had planks smashed. The fishing off Worthing is mainly for cod and herring in the winter and sole in the spring and it is good enough to support many full time fishermen. They only have to stop in the summer when the weed chokes their nets.

At Felpham a fishermen's group own a tractor which is used to launch the boats. The Ides and Ragless families fish along this section of the Sussex coast off Felpham, but there are also angling boats kept here. At Felpham and Bognor Regis, the tough GRP version of the local lute sterned beach boats are now used. The 18ft Bognor boat had the mould taken off the traditional wooden boat *Condor*, while there is also a smaller 16ft version.

At Bognor Regis some boats are kept at the bottom of Gloucester Road, but the main landing is just east of the pier. At high water the shingle beach here is steep, like Deal, but at low water there is a great expanse of flat sand. In fact the sea is very shallow here for several miles off. Coming ashore at low water, the boats have to be towed on a trailer to the foot of the shingle and then hauled up the last bit by a tractor pulling a wire rope through a block. Four lute sterned GRP boats are worked, one man to a boat, from Bognor pier beach. The fishermen also have a stall right by the road here so that most of the catch from the pots and trammel nets are retailed straight to the public. Inshore fishermen certainly supply the public with fresher fish than can be bought in shops.

Brighton pleasure boat landing with a party of trippers, c.1905   (Author)

Selsey Bill provides shelter from the prevailing south-west winds and the landing here is on the eastern side of the headland. This is a long-established landing and even in the sixteenth century Selsey cockles were well known. About a mile off the landing is an area known as The Park which has a clay bottom and was a favourite place for sailing ships to anchor for shelter. To service them the Selsey galley was developed. These were rather like the Cornish gigs and Deal galleys, but much larger. The Selsey galleys were up to 40ft in length and pulled eleven oars, but also had two lug sails. The galleys rotted away at Selsey after World War I, but an active fleet of a dozen decked craft still lay on moorings off the landing. Some GRP lute-sterned boats made by Youngs of Bognor Regis are amongst the boats kept here. In recent years Selsey has been developed as an urban area and the neat housing estates now reach right down to the fishermen's picturesque collection of old sheds. In 1984 the coast of Sussex between Selsey and Cliff End had more beach boats and more fishermen working off open beaches than any other stretch of the British coast.

The Isle of Wight had a whole series of beach landings from Bembridge right along the 'back of the Wight' (seaward) coast and round the Needles. A few boats are still kept at Beach End, Bembridge, which is a landing just on the eastern tip of the island on the Solent side of the Foreland. In 1923 a written account of this landing tells how fishermen laid pots for lobsters and prawns in the summer. In fine weather they went up to ten miles out, but if weather turned bad they could lose their pots. All the pots were made by fishermen in the winter. The fishermen rented a wood of willows which were cut, once the leaves had fallen, for pot making. This was the usual Isle of Wight practice and pots were still made like this at Shanklin in 1983; but at Bembridge the nets were woven and then made by hand until about 1880.

The fishermen on the Isle of Wight have no contact with the Sussex coast and had their own traditions. In 1790 Robert Wheeler of Chale, a village on the English Channel coast of the Isle of Wight, recorded how two boats took 3,000 mackerel to Portsmouth to sell them. This contact with the naval base has not surprisingly meant that the 'back of the Wight' boats were the traditional British transom sterned clinker boats. Sandown, on the eastern end of the island, once had a great herring fishery. According to local legend, drift nets were shot in Sandown Bay and then left to drift round the Foreland into the Solent. The fishermen went over-land to Seaview and went out and hauled their nets in other boats.

Moving west from Sandown, the village of Lake is said to have had beach boats, and so too did the attractive little resort of Shanklin and the village of Luccombe, although erosion has long since washed the fishermen's cottages away there. These 'back of Wight' fishing villages were all changed to resorts after the railways were built on the Island in the 1860s. The climate on this side of the Island is very mild and the Victorians came here in the winter, much as later generations flocked to the French Riviera and now Spain and the West Indies.

The climate is particularly good on the Undercliff, running from Niton to Ventnor. In 1870 a man called Blake claimed part of Mill Beach, Ventnor as his territory for operating pleasure craft. The local authorities tried to drive him away, but some five generations later the Blakes are still there. In 1964 Jim and Fred Blake joined up with Viv Spencer to found a 'firm' for hiring out boats, beach huts and deck chairs. Fred's son

Geoff also lends a hand, but this work will not support three men. Geoff goes crabbing and fishing off the beach and Jim also fishes from Steephill Cove with David Wheeler. In the winter Jim Blake builds wooden boats. Fishermen always build their own boats in this area and Jim Blake's boats are in the local tradition, except he now adds a 'Brighton' (lute) stern.

There are some boats kept at Wheeler's Bay, Ventnor, while at Bonchurch erosion has removed most of the beach so the landing is now down a private slip. In 1983 there were about six full time fishermen on the 'back of Wight' and about forty men working boats part time. In beach fishing there are endless disputes between full- and part-time fishermen. In addition, the beach fishermen can only go a few hours' steaming from their landings and they deeply resent decked craft (which can stay out at sea for long periods) working inshore. In some cases the beachmen protect their living by cutting 'cowboys' (outsiders) gear. On the Island there is a long standing unwritten law that each fisherman only works in one area and does not overlap with his neighbour.

Just to the west of Ventnor is the tiny Battery Cove where in the 1950s two fishermen, the 'Ventnor Pirates', worked a boat. They gave up and in 1970 Andy Butler started to work a 17ft GRP coble potting with his wife Enid. Andy Butler was not from a fishing family and approached the work with a very open mind. He was influenced by reading about American beach boats and recognised that even the arrival of low-powered Seagull outboards did not call for any change from the traditional 15ft clinker open boat. But once high powered outboards arrived on the market, a radically different type of craft could allow them to work more gear.

Andy Butler asked Q Boats of Fishbourne to make him the 18ft GRP tri-hulled boat *Ezy Ryder* which is capable of 25 knots. With wider working space he has redesigned his gear so that he now handles 100 pots instead of 40. The traditional 'back of Wight' boats only worked 24 pots and needed two men, one rowing and one hauling. Of course Andy, and now his son David with him, have a powered winch for hauling. In three years Andy Butler has only been swamped in his boat once, and that was in a force nine after dredging for oysters in the Solent. However, on another occasion, when caught in a gale west of St Catherine's Point, he returned home safely loaded with pots. Like all beach men he has to pick his weather, and the strong tides around St Catherine's Point mean that he cannot put his gear down on a spring tide. The only disadvantage of the *Ezy Ryder*'s beamy flat hull is that it is liable to become swamped when coming ashore. This problem is solved by approaching the beach at 15–20 knots and letting the boat literally slide up the sand. On one occasion she slid 24ft out of the water and up on to the ladders where she is normally kept.

Most of the tiny coves on the Undercliff can only be reached across private land. There is still one boat at Woody Bay, but Puckaster cove is deserted because no one can get down to it. In 1900 there were fourteen boats at Puckaster and some cottages and huts which have now been eroded away. Puckaster is said to be the safest of all the 'back of Wight' beach landings. The channel, like all the other coves, had to be cleared of stone every year by hand, and a breakwater was constructed to protect it from the south-west. Sometime early this century the estate manager decided the breakwater need not be kept up at the shoreward end. The result was that the sea got behind it and destroyed the landing.

Nearly down to St Catherine's Point is the tiny beach landing of Castle Haven. The landowning family here have a longstanding and successful agreement with the boat owners that in return for using the beach, they keep the approach lane clear. This lane was laid out wide enough for two waggons to pass in the days when ships discharged here with coal. The breakwater at Castle Haven is also kept up voluntarily. It is two lines of posts with stones piled between them. This was how the first medieval harbours were started and these progressed on to stone masonry walls.

On the west side of St Catherine's Point, boats are said to have worked from Rocken End, while Blackgang Chine was one of the places from which the Wheeler family worked boats. The term chine means a deep narrow ravine cutting into the cliff. At Blackgang the soft black cliff which rises some 200ft is constantly being eroded away, mainly by streams causing landslides in wet weather. Most of Blackgang Chine has actually gone into the sea, and the coast has moved back at least 300ft in the last century. At Chale houses are slowing falling into the sea and the cliff is dotted with the remains of the most recent fall.

The Wheelers used to have to haul their boats up the cliff on ladders made of blackthorn which was oily and let the boats slip. From the top of Blackgang there is an impressive view of the crumbling cliffs of West Wight, a very inhospitable place to work a boat from. Nonetheless, Chale Bay was a great mackerel fishing centre. Fish were

A Back of the Wight mackerel boat at Blackgang Chine, 1910. Most of the men are Wheelers or their relations (Jim Richards)

114

caught with 250 fathom seine nets worked from 'back of Wight' mackerel boats. These were a larger version of the pot boats and had five men to a boat, four rowing and one handling the net. There were four mackerel boats kept in Chale Bay and one each from Shanklin and Sandown came round for the season. The crews of these boats sometimes lived under the boats, which they pulled up on to the beach.

The Wheelers of Blackgang once caught two shoals in their seine and landed 18,000 mackerel. The last large haul was 10,000 mackerel in the early 1950s which was just before the fishery died out. This had been a summer activity and between February and April prawns were caught in 'withie' pots which fetched the top prices on Billingsgate Market. This was a long established custom, as in the records of Robert Wheeler in 1797 there is mention of him sending a basket of prawns to a London salesman.

When Jim Richards followed his father and grandfather in fishing off Atherfield Point in 1942 there were twelve boats here. It was a difficult place to work from because, like the other Chale Bay landings of Ladder Chine and Whale Chine, the boats had to be dragged up the cliff by a hand capstan. This was particularly difficult in wet weather because the men slipped when walking round the capstan. Even when the boats were clear of the beach and the catch had been carried to the cliff top, the work had only just begun. Jim Richards then had to load up his bicycle and cycle six miles over the hills to put the prawns on the train at Ventnor Station to send them to Billingsgate. In later years Jim Richards got a car so that he could operate a trawler in the Solent and later on he joined in the great oyster bonanza. Jim Richards was the last full time fisherman working a boat off Atherfield and actually used the landing for thirty-four years. In 1983 his old 14ft boat *David*, built in about 1930, and then the last traditional 'back of Wight' pot boat, lay derelict on the cliff top, while his cousins' two boats were still kept about 50ft up the cliff and were hauled by motor winch.

Grange Chine was another landing and a few boats are still kept at Brook where the fishermen's cottages remain beside the lane down to the Chine. In the 1920s eight boats worked from here. Some had a spritsail and foresail rig, which was usual for the Isle of Wight boats. Sail was used on the Brook boats because they were going three miles out to the lobster grounds. Those which just worked inshore were rowed. In the 1930s a standing lug was fitted, but full-time fishing finished here when World War II started.

Freshwater Bay is the only really sheltered place on western Wight and some boats even lie on moorings under West Cliff. The Bay beach, like so many landings, now has a concrete sea defence wall round it, but there is a slipway used by boats. Round the end of the Needles, on the north of the Island, a family worked boats off the beach at Colwell Bay and had beach huts to let to visitors.

Back on the coast of Hampshire, there are skiffs let out for hire off Bournemouth beach. Swanage was the first of the Dorset landings, but decked vessels, some owned by Poole fishermen, now use moorings off here in the summer. Round St Alban's Head, facing due south-west, is the beach landing of Chapman's Pool. There are no roads down to this tiny cove at the cliff foot, but a few boats are kept here, some in boathouses.

Further west there is a landing in Worbarrow Bay at the ghost village of Tyneham. This area of the Purbeck Hills has been taken over as an army training ground. The public are only allowed in when no gunnery training is taking place. Worbarrow Bay,

A boat ashore in Scratchells Bay near the Needles, 1890. Birds' eggs were collected here to sell
(Hilton Matthews)

with its ruined houses and landing slip is more like an abandoned Shetland *haaf* station than a beach landing in southern England. Beach landings tend to be very public places; solitude is usually only found out on the open sea.

The white chalk cliffs lining Worbarrow Bay make it an attractive place, but it does face south-west, making it open to the prevailing wind, although the Isle of Portland on the horizon offers some shelter. There are no elderly inhabitants in the empty silent Tyneham; their place is taken by a notice board. On this it states that at the turn of the century Worbarrow Bay fishermen used to net 5–6,000 mackerel in one catch. While this was dragged ashore someone walked up to the main village of Tyneham and sent a telegram to a Wareham fish dealer asking him to send a cart over. Lobsters and crabs were caught in pots woven by the fishermen from willow saplings known locally as 'withies'.

Lulworth Cove has a narrow entrance through chalk cliffs which forms a natural harbour. Although boats are kept on the beach the larger ones lie on moorings. A few registered fishing boats are kept on Weymouth Bay beach, although most of the fishing boats here work out of Weymouth harbour. Beyond this are the towering cliffs of the Isle of Portland which is joined to the rest of Dorset by Chesil Beach. Portland juts out into the English Channel and forces the tide round its southern end at speeds of up to 8 knots. This forms the infamous Portland Race, the tide race off Portland Bill. It would

116

seem an impossible place to try and work open boats off the sheer cliff, but the turbulent waters attract bass and mullet as well as lobster and this makes it worth working off the east shore off Portland. The men use old cranes or 'whims' from the stone quarry and lower their boats over the sheer rock face and into the sea below. The cranes seem to have been introduced in 1914 when the fishermen were forced to abandon the cove at Church Ope because it was filled in with the waste from the stone quarries.

Working off the cliff in the eddies and shanks of the terrible race calls for very detailed knowledge of local conditions. To be caught in one of the steep white breaking overfalls in a small open boat can be fatal. The men have to work in the slack water which appears at certain states of the tide. The race usually stays far off shore, particularly in a westerly, and then it is usually safe to work close inshore. However, in a south or east wind the race moves closer to the Bill and the boats are never launched at such times.

The main crane-launching site is just a few hundred yards east of the Bill. There was a wooden crane here, like the one at the next landing, but this was chopped down in a feud between fishermen. The present iron crane, put there in 1977, is owned by Brian Charles and his son John who both work boats from here. Brian Charles followed in his father's footsteps when he started fishing off the Bill in 1948.

The season for fishing off the Bill starts in March and usually ends in September, but can go on to November. The men use both single pots and strings for lobster and crab, and rods along the edge of the race for bass, but if a shoal of bass or mullet is spotted they use seine or gill nets. For bass fishing with rods a very fast boat is best. John Charles has a 16 footer capable of 26 knots which has been very successful. A really good day's fishing with this method is about 60 lbs of bass, averaging 8 lbs a fish.

Fishing from the Bill almost died out around 1970, but since then the number of boats has increased. The numbers vary from one season to the next, but in 1981 some sixteen boats were working off the Bill. The following season seven boats were in regular use.

The beach boat type unique to Chesil Beach is the double-ended clinker lerret. There is a much repeated story about the origin of the lerret being a copy of a boat seen in the Gulf of Venice by a Portland master of a Weymouth ship. It seems a highly unlikely story, part of the folklore which was such a strong part of all rural communities. The lerret is more probably part of the Norse ship-building tradition which has been evolved to suit the conditions on this part of the Dorset coast.

Chesil is an Old English word for shingle and the Beach has been piled up over the centuries by the tide so that there is a bank of stone running for about eleven miles. Behind Chesil Beach is a huge brackish lagoon called the Fleet. The Beach is so high that in the past 200 years it has only been broken through by the sea twice, once in 1824 and again in 1942. Before the Ferry Bridge was built in 1825 Portland was a remote place and the Prevention Service found it almost impossible to suppress smuggling here and on the Beach.

On Portland, Chesil Beach and the 'back of Wight' the smugglers bought their cargoes in the Channel Islands. The 19–22ft six-oar lerrets were used for the seventy to eighty mile free trade trips from Alderney. Sails were used for these long distances, first spritsail and later lug. Like most beach boats the mast and sails were kept to a length that could be stored inside the boat when they were hauled ashore.

After the smuggling era ended sails gradually dropped out of use. There was little need for sail then because the lerret's main work was seine netting for shoals of mackerel, which the tide stream pushed in close to the Beach from April to October. The Beach was divided up into areas which belonged to 'companies'. A written agreement of 1792 shows that the mackerel fishing by companies was already a highly organised affair. Each company had a lookout on the Beach who signalled when a shoal was approaching; the rest of the men then came across the lagoon in special flat bottomed boats known as Fleet Water Trows. The lerret was then slid down the shingle on its oars. The steep beach and fierce currents created strong undertows and the lerrets had to be buoyant enough to get through this. The lerret is beamier and deeper in the after section to take the weight of the seine nets.

Before 1911 20ft six-oar lerrets were normally worked by a dozen men, some rowing and others handling the shore end of the net. After this a small seine net was introduced which could be worked by about eight men and this led to a switch to a 17ft four-oar lerret.

The large 20ft lerret was also popular during the nineteenth century because they were used for salvage work. Even after the herring fishing finished in December and most of the boats were turned upside down under the lee at the back of the Beach, each company kept a lerret ready to deal either with rescue or salvage to a ship which every winter found itself driven ashore. The lerret's reputation as being suitable as a lifeboat was because of their ability to survive in the terrible breakers on Chesil Beach. In 1843 the

A four-oar lerret at Chesil with the Isle of Portland in the background, 1981   (Author)

118

Government had an 18ft lerret built at Weymouth and placed it at Atherfield on the Isle of Wight as a lifeboat. A similar lerret was placed at Brook and like the Atherfield boat was involved in several successful rescues.

In this century the lerret has gradually declined in number, but the type is still in use. In October 1973 Eric McKee found eleven lerrets on Chesil Beach, working from East Beckington, Parkwall, Wyke Regis and Chesil. The six-oar *Christina* had just been rebuilt and the four-oar *A Blessing Too* was built by H. J. Merrit the previous year. On my visits to Chesil Beach in 1981 and 1983 the lerrets and trows on the Fleet still survived, but the square ended Chesil boats seemed to be more popular. These have the same bow as the lerret but have a transom stern, which is more suitable for an outboard than a pointed stern. The square ended boats are mainly used for lining and crabbing; most seem to have been built by Nobby Clark on Portland. Like the lerret, this type has a single throle on which a 'copse' oar is permanently fixed. This type of oar remains in place while landing and the oars can be released without the problem of them falling overboard when the pots are hauled.

Because of the force of the wind the boats are tethered down with baskets or buckets of shingle when they are on the beach. Flat stones with holes are used to weigh the bottom of the seine net down. The superstition is still observed that a boat should not put to sea without a stone with a natural hole fixed into the bow. In 1983 the square ended *Sea Rover* at East Beckington had her lucky stone and the *Lisa* at Burton Bradstock, a small landing just beyond the end of the famous beach, also had one.

Although flanked by sandy cliffs, Burton Bradstock has the same steep shingle beach and wicked undertow as Chesil Beach. Looking at it, one is reminded that the dangers of working off a beach are far greater than working out of a harbour. If a gale suddenly gets up then the beachmen are cut off from the safety of the beach by the breakers. Over the centuries countless beachmen have been drowned within sight of their homes. Even with lifeboats and other rescue services the danger is always there, and a sudden wind change can see the boats having a terrible battle to get back, while the womenfolk ashore suffer real anxiety waiting to see if their men's boats land in safety.

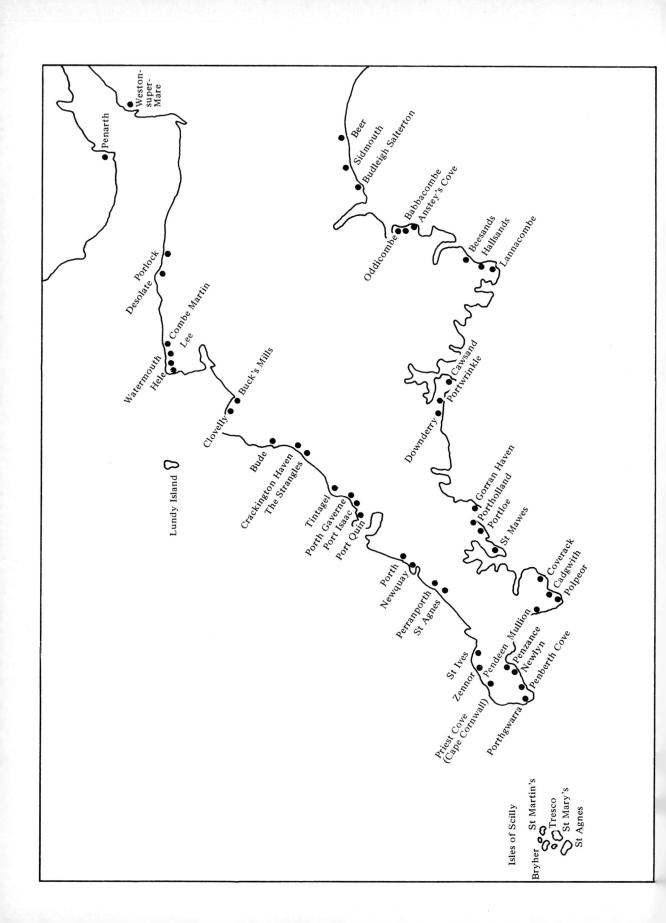

Penarth

Weston-
super-
Mare

Beer
Sidmouth
Budleigh Salterton

Babbacombe
Anstey's Cove
Oddicombe

Beesands
Hallsands
Lannacombe

Porlock
Desolate

Combe Martin
Lee
Watermouth
Hele
Buck's Mills
Clovelly

Cawsand
Portwrinkle

Downderry

Bude
Crackington Haven
The Strangles

Lundy Island

Gorran Haven
Portholland
Portloe
St Mawes

Tintagel
Porth Gaverne
Port Isaac
Port Quin

Coverack
Cadgwith
Polpeor

Porth
Newquay

Perranporth
St Agnes

Pendeen Mullion
Penzance
Newlyn
Penberth Cove

St Ives
Zennor

Priest Cove
(Cape Cornwall)
Porthgwarra

Isles of Scilly

St Martin's
Tresco
St Mary's
St Agnes

Bryher

Chapter 7
The Atlantic Fringe

The coast of Devon and Cornwall is a series of bays and coves split up by rocky headlands. With plenty of stone available locally, it has been possible to build many harbours in the sheltered parts of this beautiful coast, but beach landings remain in many of the smaller bays. Heading west along the English Channel, the first two beach landings are Seaton and Beer. On visiting Seaton in 1981 it proved to be a pleasant family resort, but no sign of working beach boats. However in the era of sail the Newtons, Snells, Welches and Wilkins worked 25ft two-masted luggers off Seaton beach. These boats conformed to a pattern found in various forms throughout the west country. They were straight-stemmed and had a transom stern.

Beer is well known in maritime history circles because it was the last place in Britain to have three-masted luggers. The beaches on this east Devon coast are steep shingle, not unlike the Sussex beaches, and the sailing luggers seem to have retained the clinker hull here, perhaps because their basket-like qualities allowed them to survive the constant strain imposed before they could be hauled clear of breaking seas. The Beer luggers of about 1900 were from 20–28ft long and the third mast was only stepped amidships when they were well clear of the beach and running or reaching. These three-masters last raced in 1914, and their final demise was sealed when higher fish prices in World War I resulted in the first engines being fitted into Beer luggers. Within two years all the larger Beer boats had engines, and the last three-master was broken up in 1918.

The beach at Beer is protected from the prevailing south-westerly winds by the 426ft high Beer Head, which makes it a reasonably sheltered landing, better than the exposed beach at Seaton; and there is good fishing ground within reasonable distance of the beach. The luggers used to go trawling on The Tenants, a piece of ground a few miles south of Beer Head. There are also some lobster and crab grounds near the landings which provide an extra bit of income to supplement other forms of fishing; so Beer continues as a commercial fishing centre. The fishermen here have followed a modern trend by co-operating in marketing their catch through a voluntary fishermen's association. A feature of the present fleet of about a dozen boats is that the boats have wheel shelters right forward in the bows. The first of these wheel shelters was fitted in the 1950s. At that time there were three hand crab capstans at the bottom of Sea Hill, all now replaced by motor winches, but the magnificent Washbourne Memorial Fisherman's Capstan is still in place at the top of the hill.

Seven miles west of Beer Head there is a beach landing at the family and retirement resort of Sidmouth. The landing is at the eastern end of the beach where the River Sid filters into the sea through the shingle below the impressive red cliffs which rise sharply to over 500ft. An 1820 print of Sidmouth shows the elegant houses along the seafront of this fashionable resort and includes the workaday scene of a trading sloop discharging cargo on the beach and open three-masted fishing luggers. These luggers were very high out of the water and had deep draught. They do not seem to have been good sailers and the fishermen said it was 'better to row than to reef'. This did not stop the Sidmouth men from sailing long distances, and some took their 20ft boats as far as Kent to fish. The men lived under the tiny foredecks. In about 1890 thirty luggers and more small boats worked off the beach. Two of the luggers were used for tending passing shipping and bringing coal ashore.

Sidmouth's sailing fishermen have been particularly well recorded, firstly by the marine painter Robert C. Leslie, who moved here in 1854 and became a great friend of Harry Conant who owned and worked the 14ft foresail and mizzen lugger *England's Rose*. Leslie realised fully just how dangerous the working lives of the beach fishermen were. He watched with admiration as the Sidmouth luggers returned from the sea in strong onshore winds when a spring tide added a wicked breaking crest to the sea. The luggers were guided in with great skill and dodged the worst of the seas before they came creaming in through the breakers to crash ashore on the hard shingle beach.

A writer who became attracted to Sidmouth was Stephen Reynolds, who was twenty-five years old when he came here first in 1906. Reynolds took lodgings with Bob Woolley, a fisherman, with the intention of gathering background material for a novel. The seemingly romantic life of the fisher folk had been a great source of inspiration for nineteenth century literature. This started with smugglers' yarns such as Sir Walter Scott's *Antiquary*, which turned Auchmithie into 'Musselcrag' and by the end of the century every stretch of coast had its fictional smuggling hero. Reynolds turned his notes (after changing the name Woolley to Widgers) about the sheer physical hard work and ordinary living conditions ashore into a factual book, *A Poor Man's House*, which, when published in 1908, brought him immediate literary acclaim.

By that time Reynolds was living with the Woolleys at Hope Cottage, Sidmouth and went on to write *Alongshore* (1910) and more books about fishing life. He was by that time living and working as an ordinary fisherman and was deeply concerned about the poverty and disease which inflicted the families ashore. He sought to improve living conditions by raising the fishermen's income and he became their champion and fought the activities of the 'middle men'. He encouraged the introduction of better sailing boats and then the addition of engines. This work led him to be appointed in 1913 to a committee enquiring into the state of inshore fisheries; a year later he became Resident Inspector of Fisheries for the South West area.

Reynolds waged war, not just on slum housing conditions, but on the whole class system which then gripped British society in a rigid structure. In this the beach fishermen were very much members of the 'lower orders', although they did have a personal freedom denied to most of the working class. Reynolds was just one of many social reformers who set out to destroy the class system, although he died at the early age of thirty-seven, long before the change which he sought took place.

The beachmen and their families lived, for the most part, in isolated communities scattered round the coast, but they have not escaped any of the changes which have affected the whole country. The industrial revolution almost ruined many beach fishermen; not only did the steam drifters and trawlers flood the markets with cheap fish, but the trawlers particularly came close inshore and worked out the inshore grounds. In the inter-war years, between 1918 and 1939, most inshore fishing communities were in a state of decline, but during this period social attitudes changed dramatically, leading to the creation of the Welfare State in the later 1940s. This had a profound effect on inshore fishing because the state, through the White Fish Authority, advanced capital for men to buy new boats. Also, even more important, it paid unemployment benefit when they could not go to sea. Inshore fishermen were given the unique position of being able to draw payment on a daily basis.

The Welfare State's support has worked well for inshore fishermen because it has taken away the hardship while at the same time leaving the fishermen with an independent way of life. There are other financial pressures on fishermen, however, as they still have to find and land a saleable catch in order to keep in business.

Other pressures on fishermen have come from the sheer number of people who wish to use the beaches for relaxation. Councils who wish to promote their seafronts for the use of visitors often discourage boats. At Sidmouth the little fleet now operates from the eastern end of the beach, with gear stores behind the car park out of sight of the visitors. About five boats are used for fishing, the largest being S. Bagwell's *Albatross*. All are open with a forward wheel shelter and these Sidmouth boats tend to be very high sided, just like the old sailing luggers. The luggers and wooden boats built later for both Beer and Sidmouth were built at Exmouth.

The next resort westward along the coast is Budleigh Salterton which the Victorian artist Sir John Millais used as the setting for his famous painting *The Boyhood of Raleigh*, a natural choice as this Elizabethan adventurer's home was in the neighbouring village. The beach landing at Budleigh Salterton in the opening years of this century was under the shelter of the West Cliff.

The beach landings of east Devon from Beer to Budleigh Salterton are much more exposed to the south-west winds than the landings in south Devon. In south Devon, around Babbacombe Bay and Tor Bay, the climate is very mild all the year round and this area was steadily built up from the Victorian period onwards as resorts. Babbacombe Cove and the adjoining Oddicombe beach face east and, being enclosed by high cliffs, are a virtual sun trap. Today all this area is a family holiday centre, but in the nineteenth century Babbacombe was a beach landing. In the 1950s the winches and ladders over which the fishing boats were hauled up the beach were still there, but when I visited the cove in 1979 there was no sign of anything connected with beach fishing.

Babbacombe can be reached by a very steep road down the cliff, but Oddicombe was virtually inaccessible until the cliff railway and a path were constructed down to it. In the inter-war years Oddicombe was a thriving beach landing, with tripper boats running off a stage in the centre of the beach and rowing skiffs pulled up by capstan. To the south of Babbacombe, round a headland, is another bay lined by Redgate Beach and then Anstey's Cove. In the Edwardian era Anstey's Cove became popular because it was at the end of a pleasant walk from Torquay and rowing skiffs were hired out here. Now

The Devon landing at Beer is well sheltered by Beer Head, c.1920   (Hilton Matthews)

this bay has pedal boats for hire and the whole area around Hope's Nose has been engulfed by urban Torquay.

The next large bay after Tor Bay is Start Bay and at the western side of this are the beach landings of Beesands and Hallsands. In about 1885 smacks, fitted with fish wells, from the Hamble River started cruising along the Devon, Cornish and Irish coasts, buying lobsters, crab and a few crayfish. Previously these had been supplying the London market from Norway and Brittany. The usual practice was for a smack to anchor off north Hallsands and then hoist a red ensign as a sign that they were ready to start buying. The local crabbers then went out to their kegs (store pots) and ferried the contents out to the smack. The crabs were sent up on to the smack's deck in bushel baskets and the men then moved around the boats walking on the crabs, taking no notice of the awful crunching sound. Once loaded, the smack moved on to Beesands where the same buying routine took place.

The boats used at Start Bay were 16ft long, transom sterned and rigged with spritsail and a foresail. A report in 1883 said that Hallsands and Beesands fishermen trained Labrador dogs to swim out with a piece of wood towing a light line. These lines were attached to heavier rope which the men used to fasten to the boats' sterns so that they could be hauled ashore. The type of pots used in the west country had the entrance hole in the middle of the top. These were sometimes called 'ink pots' and the advantage was that there was no door to be opened and the fishermen could just reach in.

124

In the late nineteenth century contractors building the new Naval Docks at Plymouth received permission to dredge sand and gravel from Start Bay. The Hallsands fishermen protested that work would undermine the foreshore and when the mooring ropes were first laid for the suction dredger, the whole village turned out to drag them away shouting 'Us'll all go to prison together'. This proved only a temporary setback, however, because the fishermen lacked the education and ability to organize an effective pressure group to halt the dredging.

Between 1900–4 many hundreds of tons of sand and gravel were dredged up from the seabed at Hallsands with the result that the foreshore started to slide into the sea. The worst erosion took place during a bad storm in 1917, and part of South Hallsands was washed away. The boats moved to North Hallsands, but this dropped from twenty-two boats in 1900 to only a handful in 1922 when the last buying smack called from the Hamble. The Hallsands crabbers and those used in Hope Cove in west Devon were built by Chant at Salcombe, and kept to the spritsail rig until motors were introduced in the 1920s. Boats are still launched off several Devon beaches including Lannacombe, but Beesands is the main commercial landing.

The Cornish beach landings are mostly tucked away in coves. The hamlet of Portholland has two coves at the foot of tall cliffs on Veryan Bay. The wide beach at Portholland East has a windlass put there for pleasure boats, but in 1982 there had been no commercial fishing within living memory. At Portholland West one boat (FH 267) was hauled out, but there was no commercial fishing and one elderly local complained

Ansteys Cove at Torquay seems to be developed as a landing solely for the holiday trade which was expanded in the Edwardian era. The hiring out of bathing machines and boats was the summer occupation of many beachmen   (Hilton Matthews)

'They are all land folk', meaning the present people living there. At the tiny landing at Portloe, on the west shore of Veryan Bay, the story was much the same. The landing was actually chained off so that everyone had to pay to use it. Three of the boats here in 1982 were used for potting, netting for ray and angling. However in 1910 when schooners came in to discharge on the beach, there were over forty open fishing boats here, and local men remembered fourteen boats working from here in the 1930s, but 'that was before holiday lets and house sales to "up country" folk'.

One of the most active Cornish beach landings seems to be Cadgwith, in a cove under the lee of the Lizard. There were ten lobster and crab boats working from here in 1982, all very modern GRP hulls, mostly with forward wheel shelters. The Cornish fishermen seem to have accepted GRP hulls far quicker than beachmen on the south and east coast of England. The reason for this may be that the traditional wooden boats of Cornwall were usually carvel (planks end-on-end so that the sides were flat). The change to GRP hulls, which from the mid 1960s were cheaper than wooden ones, meant that they did not have to accept a boat with a different appearance.

I am indebted to John McDonald for seeking out the more isolated landings in Cornwall. Down on the Lizard, the most southerly point in England, fifteen boats are kept near the slip in tiny Polpeor Cove, but only four men are fishing full-time. The main fishing is netting for ray, turbot and round fish and lining for conger, ling and pollack. John Marshall, owner of the *Margaret*, uses a smaller boat with an outboard for bass because 'the diesel would frighten them over rough ground'.

The cove at Cadgwith, Cornwall. Note the seine boat hauled up on the left   (Osborne Studio)

Mullion's Cove before the harbour was built   (Osborne Studio)

The cove at Mullion is protected by a wall originally built at the expense of Viscount Clifton in 1887, but the boats are still hauled out because of the tremendous Atlantic swell which comes boiling in round the Lizard Point once the wind gets in the south. Eddie Munday of Mullion recalled that before World War I there were five companies operating in the lucrative pilchard fishing from the cove. The companies had a 'huer' or lookout on the cliff top watching for the dark patches of the pilchard shoals approaching across the sandy sea bottom. The shoals came in from the Atlantic in about September and split up north and south at Land's End. The Mullion people also watched from Mullion's Island, looking out across Mount's Bay, and if they saw the mackerel drivers (luggers) from Newlyn, this was another sign that the shoals were approaching the Lizard. The luggers collected some of the pilchard caught by the seine boats and took them back to Newlyn.

Once the 'huer' spotted the shoals, he signalled down to the fishermen with two gorse bushes held aloft; this was the sign for the 36ft open seine boats with eight men to be launched and go to sea. Once at sea, the 'huer' continued to give directions by waving and bowing in the direction for the boat to head; turning his back on the boat was a sign for them to turn inshore. Each company boat had its own 'stem' or section of the coast which was allotted at the beginning of the season by a draw. There was no poaching between the companies for another boat's water.

If a boat managed to get its huge seine net round a shoal the whole mass was dragged on to the beach and then all the company shareholders had to transport the pilchard to the curing houses or cellars (the one at Mullion is now a private house) where the oil was extracted and the fish salted. Much of it was exported to Italy and other catholic countries where it was eaten on fast days.

The last shoot of pilchard at Mullion was in 1921, which was about the last time this happened in Cornwall. Since then lobstering and crabbing have been the mainstay for boats. In 1983 five boats were working from Mullion, but with the sea rolling into this cliff-lined cove it is a very dangerous place to work from. John Pascoe of *Patrice* said that the swell considerably limits the days that it is safe to go to sea.

The very western tip of England is the Penwith Peninsula, which has no harbours between Mount's Bay round Land's End to St Ives. The Atlantic swell rolls in and hammers against miles of Cornish cliffs so that the only places that boats can be launched from are little more than clefts in the granite cliffs. The village of Porthcumo has two tiny landings at Penberth Cove and Porthgwarra. At Penberth Cove the hand capstan is suspended on a 24ft beam between two rock pillars. This worked fine when about fifteen men fished from the Cove and there were always enough 'bodies' to man the capstan. When Dave Chapple started full time fishing in 1952 there were so few men that sometimes he took half an hour to get his *Tunny* up the slip. Fishermen at Penberth were very pleased when the Penzance dentist Dave Motton, who kept a little boat here and loved the place, fitted the first motor winch in 1950.

Dave Chapple first used a set of hooked feathers jigged in the water for mackerel in about 1946. The Cornish men had seen the Scottish boats using this technique. In 1959 the Penberth men started to do really well at mackerel fishing. The Newlyn fisheries officer put Penberth men in touch with the Fish Organisation Society and with their help they formed the Penberth Winch Society and ran their own lorry. In the mid 1960s Penberth Cove was once placed in the top ten mackerel ports in Britain and this was achieved by only a dozen men. Their success did not go unnoticed, for before long big purse seiners began to move in on the Cornish mackerel. However in 1982 there were still eleven boats, all about 16ft long, fishing from Penberth Cove.

In the past the men of Penberth Cove fished in the summer and became farmers, growing chiefly flowers, in the winter. In 1983 seventy-three year old John Henry Chapple talked of seeing the Penberth Cove men 'shooting' a seine net for pilchard. The shoal they got was so large that Porthgwarra seine boats also came to help and it took three days to empty the net. In the end the weather broke and the rest of the catch was lost. Still, John Henry's father took £90 for his share, which was more than he earnt for the rest of his year's work.

A 24ft Penberth seine boat was owned by a local parson and squire and because they had a financial stake in the pilchard fishing, the squire ordered that no lobster pots were to be set near the cove after the end of August. This resulted in a major local row between the seining company and the Jackson family who were lobster fishermen. In the end the Jacksons moved to Porthgwarra and the Chapple families moved into the empty cottages at Penberth.

The Porthgwarra landing is so small that it is hardly visible from the sea at high tide. It is just a tiny slip leading up to a man-made arch cut in the rock. There are several of

128

these holes in rock faces, and they were made by St Just miners so that horses and carts could collect seaweed for the farms. Old pictures show eighteen boats at Porthgwarra, but it seems that men had to cover a wide area to get a living, often having to row eight miles out to the Wolf Rock.

There was also a seine boat at Porthgwarra and in the autumn the people were constantly watching for pilchard. At night the gorse was even fired as a sign that the shoals had arrived. Although only about eight men went out in the seine boats, the whole district helped to get the catch in to the fish cellars. In an age when most people lived on the edge of real poverty, the pilchard shoals were the only chance to make any extra cash.

The last full-time fisherman at Porthgwarra was Dick Rawlings, who retired in about 1967, and now only four boats are kept here, of which *Our Maggie* and *Snow Goose* are fished part-time. Mrs Rawlings acts as harbour-master for the St Aubyn Estate.

These landings on the very tip of England are open to the full fury of the Atlantic. There is none more open that Sennen Cove, just east of Land's End. In spite of its name it really is not a cove at all, but just a slightly sheltered side of Whitesand Bay. Off this rugged coast is the lone lighthouse on the Longships Rock. The first lighthouse was built here in 1776 and for 200 years all the stores and men were taken out from Sennen. The main village of Sennen is on the cliff top, inland. The people here are the 'Over Hillers' and in the past were quite separate from the fishing community of about a hundred people down beside the cove. The actual landing is slightly protected by a breakwater, but it is still very exposed and an exacting place to work a boat from. Before World War I there were two-masted luggers used for crabbing from here and also for undertaking a bit of salvage. Ocean-going sailing ships were sometimes unable to fix their position when coming in from the Atlantic and consequently they just ran in to this inhospitable coast.

Salvaging from wrecks was not without its dangers, for in 1886 the Sennen luggers were returning deeply loaded from a wreck off Cape Cornwall when a man was washed overboard from one of them, and was never seen again. However, a 'good wreck' was looked on as being a godsend on the Cornish coast. A Swedish barque which was wrecked off Sennen in 1913 is still remembered with affection by the older generation because she supplied them with coal and fire bricks for years.

Before World War I there were six companies working Whitesand Bay for pilchard and some large catches were made here, but the pilchards were becoming rarer even then. The 'huer' had a hut on the cliff top which fell down during World War I and the fishery was not revived here. However crabbing luggers were used for a few more years. They were hauled up the slip by a huge wooden capstan, like the one at Penberth, housed in the Round House. Although the conditions are very rough around Land's End, the fishing is good. When Henry Hards started fishing from Sennen in 1949 he and his brother could earn a living working about fifty pots from the 25ft crabber *Henry & John*. Fishing was good in the 1950s and 1960s when five large boats worked from Sennen. In 1982 there were still five boats working from the Cove, but they were smaller and below 19ft long. Most of the boats here, like *Clair*, which belongs to the lifeboat coxswain, Morris Hutchinson, are GRP. Pulled up on the sand they look very small to go out into the huge rollers which come crashing on the beach at Whitesand Bay.

Sometimes in March, huge shoals of mullet appear in Whitesand Bay. The men of Sennen Cove turn out with a special net to harvest this rewarding crop. The Sennen Cove men regard the mullet as being their property and have always fought off attempts by St Just men to join in. Once a French boat came in and tried to get the shoal, but they were driven away by stoning. In about 1969 some men from Par decided to come by road with boat and nets to take some of the Whitesand mullet. Spotting the arrival of these 'trespassers', about thirty Sennen men rushed up the hill armed with knives and stones. Faced with this aggressive opposition the Par men left, but promised to return in force. This they did, but as the two forces of very angry fishermen moved towards each other ready to do battle, the Penzance police, who had also arrived in force, got between them. The Par men were obliged to retire once more, empty handed.

The exact amount of mullet landed from these shoals is a secret closely guarded by the Sennen Covers. In 1982 the mullet had not appeared for three years, but some local people suggested that before that a thousand stone was landed in a season and in the previous year four thousand stone were taken.

The landings in coves north of Whitesand Bay were used in the past by tin miners from Levant and Geevor mines. The fish were either sold when work in the mines was going through a slow patch, or salted down for winter use. The miners used their skill with explosives to blast away rocks in the channel, but these coves were still very exposed when the wind was in the north-west and north. In 1982 seventy-five year old Tom Trudgeon, who had worked in Geevor Mine, remembered that Pendeen men had luggers up to 21ft long. They used to go a long way off and about ten miles down to the Longships, after gurnard, a red fish about a foot long. The smaller pulling boats often had troubles with the strong tides. If they failed to get into the cove, they were swept down to Sennen, about eight miles away. Weather conditions on the coast have not altered in the slightest over the years. The men using the Priest's Cove on Cape Cornwall go out in open outboard boats which have to ride through huge rollers at the entrance.

Before 1914 there was a pilchard company at Pendeen and about a dozen boats were fishing from the Boat Cove. The boats were hauled by capstan and seaweed was used for the boats to run on. In the years between the wars the capstan bars broke and no one bothered to replace them. Tom Trudgeon said that the boats became increasingly heavier as they received another coat of tar each year, and the men got less inclined to haul them out. It was a classic case of the boats wearing out and not enough cash return to replace them. Consequently everyone gradually lost interest.

Around 1967 a village committee was formed to look after and develop the Boat Cove. By 1982 a new concrete slipway and huts had been built and a winch installed. Twelve boats, about half of them part time, were fishing from the Boat Cove. The number of people wanting to fish from here increased and the arrival of newcomers caused a tremendous local row.

There is no public road, only a footpath to the Boat Cove at Pendeen. This is not unusual because before the coming of cars the fishermen walked to and from work. It is also quite desirable that the more out-of-the-way places around the British coast are kept free of the tourist car. At Pendeen the farmer allowed the fishermen to use cars to get to the Cove, but in 1982 this permission, because of the increasing number of cars, was withdrawn. The gateway used by the fishermen was blocked with stone. Six fishermen

130

decided to go and remove the stones and the farmer's son tried to prevent them. A scuffle took place and he ended up in a pool of cow dung.

The west cost of Cornwall and north Devon are very exposed and only have a few beaches between miles of cliffs. Yet before the coming of road transport many of the remote coastal villages had all their coal for winter cooking and heating supplied by sailing traders on the beaches. On the Devon coast, house coal was brought ashore at Combe Martin, where there is a small beach between two rock outcrops which are under water at high tide. In the 1890s the 40-ton trading smack *Sir T. D. Acland* was owned by George Irwin of Combe Martin, while the *Olive & Mary*, owned by James Irwin of Combe Martin traded to Watermouth, a cove two miles to the west. The Irwins also owned the 54ft ketch *Jane*, which they used to trade to Lee Bay with coal in the summer. This is a fairly sheltered place because the prevailing wind is off the land for nine months of the year. However, the beach traders did not hang about in such places. At Lee Bay they put about seventy tons of coal ashore, mostly for the lighthouse, and had to get off within twenty-four hours, before the weather broke.

At Hele beach, near Ilfracombe, a ketch loaded with Welsh coal used to come ashore about once a year before World War I. This was a year's supply of household fuel for Berrynarbor. Some of these little traders were owned in the beach landing villages, but in this century the Appledore and Braunton vessels took over this work, which probably ended when the Appledore ketch *Hobah* discharged at Porth Luney Cove, Cornwall in 1937.

Peter Herbert of Bude, who was skipper of the ketch *Agnes* in the 1950s, heard the older generation of sailors reminiscing about the beach trade in the latter part of the nineteenth century. On the Devon coast men spoke of 'Us fetched into Desolation'. This was the lime kiln between the Foreland and the 'Gentleman's House' (Glenthorpe). When bound from Appledore Bar up channel in the M/V *Despatch* Peter Herbert used to keep inshore 'working the rocks' to dodge the ebb tide. When he passed Desolation he could still pick out the white kiln wall which had been painted, perhaps 120 years earlier, by coasting masters so that they could see where to go ashore.

On this coast beach trade ended when Appledore barges ceased, in the 1920s, going to Clovelly and Porlock Bay in the summer for road stone. At some Cornish beach landings, trade had finished quarter of a century before this and there is little record of it. Coal came into Crackington Haven and was taken inland by horse and butt (cart). On the more open coast, traders came ashore at The Strangles, south of Cambeak, and mooring rings have been found in the rocks. No one remembers now whether ships came ashore at The Strangles to load slate or ore.

In west Cornwall coal was discharged on the beach under the shadow of Tintagel Castle. The flat hard white sand in the cove at St Columb Porth was an ideal place to discharge. The Cornish place name Porth means literally a safe place for boats to land; it does not necessarily mean a harbour as in the equivalent English word port. The porth or cove at St Columb is only about two miles from Newquay harbour, but when everything had to be moved by horse and cart, just moving coal that extra distance was a slow and expensive operation.

On the cliffs near Newquay is the Huer's House, a reminder of the pilchard fishing industry which in the mid nineteenth century was a great money earner. There were pilchard fishing companies on this coast, as on the south coast, and it was divided into areas which 'belonged' to each company. Because of the high returns from the sale of pilchard for export in barrels, and for oil for rush lantern fuel, there was much tension over the right to take the shoals. In Perran Bay seine netting started in about 1750 and the companies were based at Perranporth. Each section of the community had its own company such as the Miners, Farmers, Union (tradesmen) and Love (a mixture of employment). As drift netting increased at sea the inshore seine netting declined, and in 1886 the last seine of pilchards was landed in Perranporth, which raised £600. Some of the Newquay companies are reputed to have taken £70,000 of pilchard in a year, but seine netting finally finished at St Ives in 1908. Now the flat sandy beaches of Newquay and Perranporth, with their huge white crested Atlantic rollers thundering in, attract surf riders and the seine boats of Cornwall have become just a part of the local history.

At St Agnes, there was sufficient trade to build a small harbour which was washed away in 1934. Incredibly there was also shipbuilding on this open coast. At Trevaunance Cove, St Agnes on the foreshore below a cliff, in front of Goonlaze mine, M. T. Hitchens & Co. built the trading schooners *St Agnes* (1873), *Goonlaze* (1874), *Trevellas* (1876) and *Lady Agnes* (1877). The *Goonlaze* and the 102ft *Trevellas*, reputed to have been one of the fastest British schooners ever built, were ocean-going ships designed for the Newfoundland trade.

Porth Gaverne was probably the busiest of all the west Cornish porths or beach ports. The cove pushes inland like a long finger between high land. It is well sheltered except when the wind is in the west and then a huge swell funnels up the cove, boiling white on the rocks on either side. The little trading smacks and ketches which came in here to load from Delabole Quarry had to put out two heavy mooring hawsers astern, one from each quarter, to stop the vessels from being thrown up the beach by the sea. Like all the beach ports the problems were ground swell which could hammer the wooden vessels to pieces on the hard bottom. At St Agnes huge blocks and tackle were rigged which were used to keep the vessels down tight so that they would not pound on the bottom when the ground swell came rolling in.

The trader *Prince Alfred* is recorded as being lost at Porth Gaverne. Apparently she rolled over and pounded during a bad gale. In 1886, 106 cargoes were handled, most by women, in this cove; throughout the Victorian era this must have been a very busy place. The trade lasted until World War I and the trading smack *Rifleman* is remembered as being the last to discharge here.

Before World War I Porth Gaverne also had some thirteen fishing boats, although Port Isaac, in the next cove, was the main fishing centre. In the herring season the whole of Port Isaac Bay was a mass of lights at night as the Cornish and East Coast boats lay to their drift nets. Once the local lugger *Kindly Light* was caught at sea in a gale when the herring in the hold shifted and she 'turned turtle'. The lugger sank and the crew of four decided to swim ashore, leaving the skipper who could not swim clinging to two oars. As the gale died, another lugger, the *Deerhound*, spotted a flock of gulls on the water which were in fact feeding on the herring out of the *Kindly Light*. On the *Deerhound* they shook the reef out of her forelug and sailed over hoping to find a shoal of fish. Instead they discovered and rescued the skipper in the water. The other men reached the shore but were later found dead of exposure on the open rocks.

Apart from the local traders and fishing boats, another force in old Porth Gaverne was the Methodist chapel. The preachers had a very strong creed of Right and Wrong. One local fisherman was strongly suspected of killing a girl he had 'got into trouble' by pushing her off the cliff above the cove. Later it was considered divine justice when the fisherman's boat was upset when returning into the cove and he just managed to swim ashore, but lost his boat and gear.

In 1981 there was still a group of boats pulled out at Porth Gaverne. The National Trust own the cove's surroundings and the Fish Cellars. These Fish Cellars needed restoring, but those at Port Isaac are still used as a lobster pot and gear store by the fishermen. At Port Quin, a very narrow cove round the headland, the small set of Fish Cellars were being converted to holiday homes.

On the north Devon coast, Buck's Mills or Bucksh has a small beach landing between rocks at the foot of the cliff. A steep track winds up from the beach and at one time donkeys were used to bring goods up, which included hard coal brought from South Wales by small sailing vessels for the lime kiln beside the track. In 1982 there were three registered boats here, and one of the sailing Buck's Mills luggers was in the Exeter Maritime Museum. They also have a similar boat from Clovelly presented by J. J. Headon whose family had her built at Appledore in 1906 for £10. This boat was small enough to be dragged down the beach at low water, while the Clovelly herring 'picarooner' were luggers of about 20ft long which were kept behind the breakwater and could only leave at high water. In the summer Clovelly boats also landed passengers from the excursion steamers.

In 1976 the North Devon Museum Trust acquired from the beach at Buck's Mills the 11ft Clovelly ledger boat *Wave*, built by Williams at Appledore in 1888. When the museum took her over the *Wave* still had the purple line painted round her which was the West country 'mourning line' for her dead owner. The usual custom at Buck's Mills on the death of their owners was to take the boats out and sink them with pebbles, but the *Wave* escaped this fate.

The *Wave* had been owned by the well known fishing family of Braund. An account in the *Exeter & Plymouth Gazette* of 1850 tells how two Braunds launched their boat to go off to assist an American brigantine in trouble in Bideford Bay in a gale. The paper described the terrible anxiety of the families watching from the cliff as 'the wailing and screams of the wives and children of the two Braunds is beyond power to express – they watched their progress up the Bay as far as they could with momentory expectation to see them "sink and rise no more„ . . .' The Braunds did however survive and managed to get the brigantine safely over the Bar into the safety of the river at Appledore.

Clovelly, with its main street falling in a series of steps some 400ft from the cliff top to the harbour, is one of Britain's major tourist show places, but it is still a living community. The local boatmen like John Glover rely very much on running trips to supplement the modest income from fishing. However, the boats still go out from the sheltered landing after lobster. Tom Braund and his son were still making the traditional west country 'inkpot' lobster pots of cane in 1983. They said these were more successful than the modern wire pots which they believed set up a vibration caused by the water moving through them.

In good weather steamers and then motor vessels from Ilfracombe and Cardiff ran excursion trips to Lundy Island, some twelve miles from Hartland Point out in the Bristol Channel. Lundy does not have a harbour and all visitors and goods have to be taken ashore from the landing beach which is sheltered by Rat Island on the south-east corner of the island. Occasionally when this beach is exposed to fresh winds, goods are landed at Jenny's Cove on the west side of Lundy.

One method of fishing which has vanished in Cornwall and Devon is the use of spears. The *Royal Cornwall Gazette* reported in 1807 that 10,000 fish were being taken by 'our spearmen' in five calm days. This is not an isolated incident because spears were used all over Britain where ever flat fish were left trapped by the falling tide in shallow pools. The use of spears declined as coastal fish stocks fell. It would seem that in Cornwall commercial spear fishing had finished by the 1890s. A spear found at Pendeen is on display at the Zennor Wayside Museum and others have been found at Cadgwith and Mousehole. The last place where spear fishing took place was at St Ives and Mousehole where it was a common sight to see half a dozen men wading in the pools spearing for fish to eat.

While this ancient method of fishing has been forgotten on the mainland, it is still continued in the Isles of Scilly, some twenty-six miles out in the open Atlantic off Land's End. In 1977 four people on Scilly used spears and one of these, Denis Jenkins of Tresco, was still using a three-pronged spear which had been made for his grandfather. When he was first given it in 1946 it did not have a handle, but eventually some suitable Oregon pine was washed ashore. Denis Jenkins needed a long handle because he often worked in up to 18ft of water. The method was to stand in the bow of a 'punt' (boat) and look down through the clear water. His record was spearing twenty-seven plaice before breakfast and in the 1920s his father quite often took twenty in an hour. This was mostly in the New Grimsby Channel, but the numbers of fish landed this way have decreased, due partly to the number of power boats in the summer season and the increase in shags which eat the young fish.

Although Scilly is surrounded by good fishing grounds, it is too far from markets to develop a fishing fleet. The same difficulty affects farming; the climate is mild and flowers particularly flourish under the shelter of high hedges, but there is the expense of a 42 mile voyage on a ferry between St Mary's and Penzance before they can start to find a market. Today tourism is the backbone of the Scillonian economy, but in the nineteenth century the only regular income for the islanders was derived from passing ships, mainly in pilotage, with occasional smuggling and salvage as well.

Compared to Cornwall, Scilly does not have a particularly ancient seafaring tradition; indeed, it is doubtful if the isles were settled before the mid-seventeenth century. Scilly is a group of low isles with sheltered beaches from which boats can be launched.

For general work within the islands, gigs were ideal, but they were not a Scillonian invention. Gigs are fast narrow pulling boats which were common in the eighteenth century as general runabouts. On the Cornish mainland, across the estuary from Falmouth in the village of St Mawes, John Peters was a noted builder of gigs. The gig he built in 1791 for a Padstow 'gentleman in Holy Orders' is now regarded as being the prototype of all the pilot gigs of Cornwall and the Isles of Scilly.

The Peters family remained the main builders of gigs over the next century and their gigs were used all round the Cornish coast at Polruan, Fowey, St Mawes, Truro,

Falmouth, Porthallow, Coverack, Penzance, St Ives, Newquay, Padstow, Port Quin, Port Isaac and Boscastle. There were also about thirty gigs in Scilly.

One of the more common uses for the gigs was for smuggling. It was 136 miles from Scilly to Roscoff which is a long way for an open pulling boat, although sails were used when there was a fair wind. The advantage of a gig was that being small, the Revenue cutters had great difficulty in spotting them at sea, and if spotted, the gigs could avoid capture by rowing up into the wind faster than the cutters could tack. Of course the sea-keeping qualities of the gigs should not be over-estimated; many were lost at sea. However the Revenue Service's main way of suppressing smuggling was to try and burn suspected gigs and outlaw the building of new ones. However, since gigs had normal employment as well, the Revenue Service only managed to ban eight-oared gigs, which effectively meant limiting them to six oars.

In the early nineteenth century many men were driven to smuggling because of the general poverty in Scilly. The practice of acting as pilots for vessels bound up Channel was already long established, but it failed to support all the people. Scilly's real salvation came in 1834 when Augustus Smith took over the lease of the Isles of Scilly from the Crown. He was a benevolent autocrat who devoted his life and wealth to improving the living conditions on Scilly. He built the Abbey, a baronial residence on Tresco, and was known as the 'Emperor'. Smith fostered new industry such as shipbuilding, but was determined to stamp out smuggling, while doing everything in his power to aid the pilots.

The St Martin's gig *Lily* in 1904. She was built in 1873 by Peters and carries the normal rig of the gigs in the Isles of Scilly while some Cornish gigs had spritsail mizzens   (Osborne Studio)

One method of placing a pilot on an incoming ship was for a gig to be launched when a ship appeared on the horizon. Usually a ship would attract more than one gig, and there would be a hard fought race to see who could get the job. The Scilly pilots also had powerful gaff cutters in which they cruised at sea waiting for ships. These pilot cutters often towed a gig which in a calm was used to get to a ship first. With gigs and cutters there was fierce competition and the gigs which always came second were sold because they simply could not earn a living for their owners. The Scillonians were also competing equally fiercely with pilots from Falmouth who were also lying out in the Atlantic waiting for ships.

In the eighteenth century the Scilly pilots administered themselves by a body called the 'Court of Twelve'. However in 1808 this right passed to Trinity House who were responsible for most of the pilotage in Britain. In 1876, because few ships were bothering to call at Scilly for a Channel pilot, Trinity House decided to reduce the number of licensed pilots. Augustus Smith ordered the pilots who had lost their licences to continue working. When some of the men who still held licences tried to have the unlicensed pilots stopped, he promptly evicted them from their houses.

There was tremendous bitterness over this in Scilly, but with the introduction of more steam ships the need for 'Scilly pilots' slowly dwindled away. St Agnes, because it was the most westward inhabited island, and the one usually spotted first by incoming ships, became the last place in Scilly where pilots operated from. The last pilot cutter working was the 40ft *Agnes* in about 1896.

When pilotage had finished many of the gigs were still carefully looked after by the Scillonians because they had been so important to them. The gigs were still used for carrying passengers and goods between the off islands and St Mary's, and there were races for them most summers. They were stored ashore in low gig houses between jobs, which meant that they lasted far longer than if they were left out. They were often blown over and smashed if left in the open. Very few gigs were owned outright by one man; the ownership was usually divided between a group who worked the gig. These shares were often held by widows and the descendants of the men who had originally bought the gig. When there was a lucrative salvage there was often a great deal of argument over the way the money was divided.

The wreck of an ocean-going ship brought in large sums of money. It was the salvage money from the wrecks which financed the building of many houses in Scilly and several of the gigs. Sometimes a ship in distress was brought into the Roadstead or in the case of one ashore on the rocks, the cargo was brought ashore. The steamer *Minnehala* which hit Scilly Rock in 1910 was loaded with everything from cars to sewing machines, but the gigs managed to swim 170 fat steers ashore which were also on board. These cattle were swum two each side of the gig from the *Minnehala* to the uninhabited island of Samson. Usually the gigs operated in fierce competition, but with this wreck several clubbed together to form a 'salvage company'. The *Sussex* was actually the first gig to reach this wreck but the *Czar* was also used to swim many cattle ashore while the *Zelda* (built in 1874 from salvage money from a steamer of that name) landed fourteen steers and a pony on Samson.

In 1919 the people on Bryher spotted the three-masted schooner *Marion G Douglas* drifting at sea. Every man on Bryher, except for three who were away, put to sea in the

136

Czar and the *Sussex*, boarded the schooner and sailed her into the Roadstead. This schooner had been abandoned off the Newfoundland coast but her timber cargo had kept her afloat. The schooner lay in the Roadstead for about six weeks, and was then sailed to Glasgow. The Bryher men had £3300 to share between them and one of the Jenkins family who had only just been released from service from World War I received £120. This was the equivalent of what he would have expected to have earned in about two years of lobster potting and other fishing activities.

Faster and reliable motor launches gradually took over all the work in Scilly during the inter-war years, but old pilots religiously guarded the gigs. On the Cornish mainland most gigs just disappeared when their use ended, except at Newquay on the northwest coast where a rowing club took over some gigs after World War I. The age of some gigs can only be estimated, but the Newquay Rowing Club's 30ft *Newquay* has documentary evidence to show she was built in 1812. They also have the *Dove*, built in 1820, and the 32ft *Treffry*, built in 1838, which is usually regarded as being the longest and fastest gig built.

These Newquay gigs had been built by Peters down at St Mawes. In about 1849 Samuel Tiddy had gone down to Scilly and started building there after serving an apprenticeship at Peters. In the late nineteenth century there were many other boatyards

The 31ft Bryher gig *Czar* painted dark green, with Bill Jenkins as coxswain with cattle alongside being swum ashore from the steamer *Minnehaha* at the back of Bryher, 1910   (Gibson)

Tom Chudleigh with the gig *Czar* at Hugh Town, St Mary's 1981. She and the *Golden Eagle* were originally kept in thatched gig houses which helped to preserve them, on the west Atlantic coast of Bryher   (Author)

in Scilly and Cornwall building and repairing gigs. Although each gig is slightly different, some were more beamy for carrying and salvage work, but there was no real difference between the gigs from Scilly and Cornwall.

In 1953 the Newquay Rowing Club was asked if it would like to buy some of the gigs remaining in Scilly. The result was the purchase of the St Martins gig *Bonnet* of 1830, the *Golden Eagle* of 1870 from Bryher, and the *Slippen* of 1830 from St Agnes. The following year the *Shah* of 1873 was purchased. These were very old boats, although still youngsters compared to the ones already at Newquay. However in the 1950s most of the Scillonian gigs were in a rather frail state as they had had little in the way of repairs since World War I. Apart from being used by soldiers during World War II, most of them had not been in the water for years. The Newquay Rowing Club found that most of the Scillonian gigs which they bought leaked and had to be rebuilt. The *Bonnet* was made slightly narrower because she was now to be used solely as a rowing gig in club races. In the working days gigs all carried sails and used them whenever possible, although they usually had to be rowed round when tacking to windward.

In 1962 only the gigs *Czar*, *Sussex*, *Klondyke* and *Campernell* remained in Scilly, but it was decided to hold a gig race in the Bank Holiday Regatta. Two retired pilots were persuaded to be coxswains although at the time few young men in Scilly had ever rowed a gig. The Agnes pilot Jack Hicks coxed the *Campernell* although she made so much water that it was almost a full-time job keeping her afloat. Pilot Hicks kept remarking that he could not understand it as the gig had never leaked before. It seems that two

138

years earlier two young men on Agnes had borrowed the *Campernell* to take flowers out to the launch which could not get in because of the heavy swell. On returning they had hit the rocks, but had never told pilot Hicks.

In the 1962 race John Jenkins, then in his eighties, took on his old place as coxswain of the *Czar*. This race caused tremendous interest in Scilly and rekindled enthusiasm for the gigs. Then next year Newquay lent the *Shah* and the *Bonnet* back to Scilly and a whole new series of gig races was started. The Scillonians also revived their use for open sea passages. The *Czar*, coxed by John Jenkins, was rowed to Penzance in ten hours. Soon there were so many people in Scilly wanting to pull an oar that there were not enough gigs available. A group got together and asked the St Mary's boat builder Tom Chudleigh to build them a new gig. Tom Chudleigh based the new gig on the *Bonnet* and set to work in a glasshouse at Well Cross in Hugh Town to build the *Serica*, the first gig built this century.

The *Serica* was launched in 1967, won her first race that year and the following year was rowed to Penzance. She was so successful that it was decided to attempt to revive the old smugglers' route and row across to France. In 1969 two attempts were made to reach Le Conquet in *Serica*, but both times the bad weather forced her back. The same year Tom Chudleigh built another new gig, the *Dolphin* for St Martins and she was followed by *Nornour* which was actually built at Looe in 1971.

Within a fortnight of her launch the *Nornour* had been rowed across to Sennen Cove and back in 24 hours. The next year the *Nornour* was rowed to Roscoff in Brittany in 37 hours, the first time a gig had made the crossing since about 1890, although in the *Nornour*'s case a fishing vessel went along as a stand-by vessel, something the old smugglers never had. They were at sea alone and in bad weather had to row continuously to keep the gigs head-on into the seas.

In 1973 the Newquay Rowing Club asked for their gigs back, but by then the Scillonians had become very attached to the old pilot gigs which had been so much a part of Scilly's past. It was agreed that if Scilly built new gigs as replacements, they could keep the old pilot gigs. To fulfil this agreement Tom Chudleigh built the *Active* in 1974, the *Good Intent* in 1975, which was financed by the landlord of the Sailor's Arms, Newquay, and the *Unity* which was completed in 1,033 man hours in 1978. Newquay returned the *Shah*, *Bonnet* and in 1980 the *Slippen*. The only Scilly gig then remaining on the mainland was the *Sussex*, which was being rebuilt after being blown over outside her gig house.

In the 1970s racing in the summer evenings became very popular, both with local people and visitors. All the inhabited off-islands had at least one gig and inter-island competition was very real. However the permanent population of the off-islands has been steadily falling and St Martins and Bryher were having trouble finding crews in the early 1980s.

The seven Scillonian gigs have followed a fashion started at Newquay of having their names painted on their bow. In the working days gigs were painted different colours, but there was no reason for them to be identified at sea. Indeed, with smuggling and rivalry between different pilots, it was often desirable not to be recognized. It is largely so that summer visitors can recognize them easier that the names have now been painted on the bow.

139

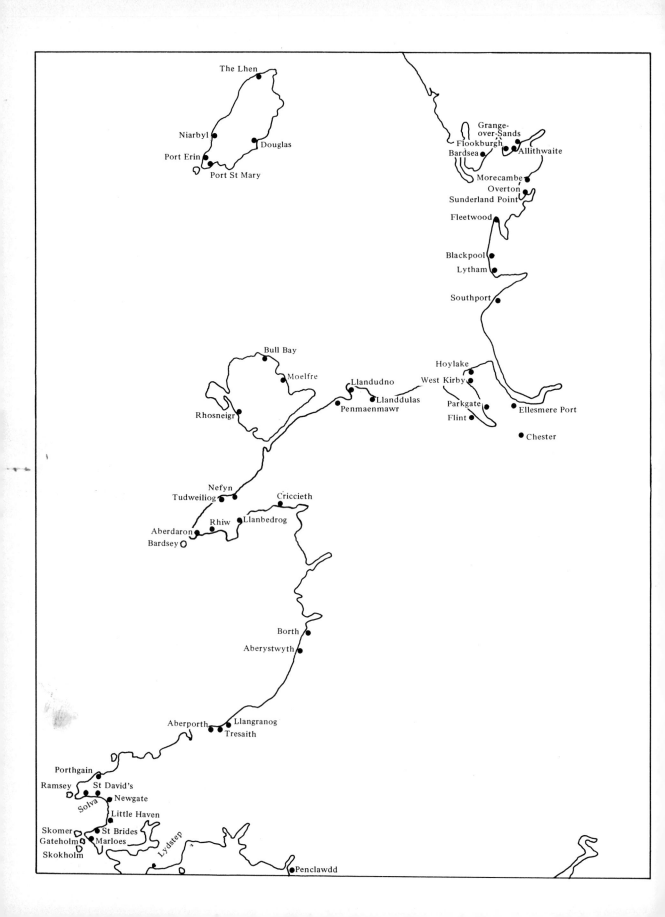

Chapter 8
The Western Shore

The Principality of Wales is a land where for many centuries fishing from small boats helped to support much of the population. On the fast flowing fresh water rivers it was the coracles which were used in pairs to net salmon, while on the six hundred miles of coast and estuary, numerous types of open boats were used for herring drifting, lining and gathering shell fish. In about 1880 nearly every fresh water river in Wales and and the bordering counties of England had coracles fishing in large numbers. After World War I the decreasing stocks of salmon caused licensing to be gradually introduced. The real demise of coracle fishing, however, was forced on most rivers by the angling clubs, which wanted to land fish for recreation rather than as part-time employment.

In Wales, inshore fishing was closely linked with grassland farming. Men worked on the land between fishing seasons. The most important fishery was the herring, which came close to different parts of the Welsh coast throughout the year. The pattern altered slightly over the centuries, but normally herring came close to the South Wales coast in the spring. These herring preferred the low salinity water close to the Pembrokeshire coast to spawn in. In Cardigan Bay the herring were landed in August and in the autumn, while in North Wales and Anglesey the herring were caught, while spawning off shore in deep water, from the autumn until January.

The herring fishing was well established in Wales during the medieval period, and became important in the sixteenth century when the use of imported salt made it possible for the fish to be exported in barrels. From then until World War I herring was the mainstay of the economy of most Welsh coastal villages. By the 1920s fresh herring was being sent by rail to English industrial towns, but the number of men employed in the fishery was falling rapidly.

Most coastal villages had salt houses where fish was packed in barrels. However, the practice in Wales was for travelling salesmen, called 'carriers' in Aberporth and 'croeswrs' in Nefyn, to buy the fish from landing boats and then sell them to farmers for curing or smoking. Each salesman worked for just one boat. In this way herring provided cheap protein food and a money earner to coastal districts.

The tiny bay at Tenby in the south is one of the most sheltered places from the prevailing westerlies blowing in the Atlantic rollers. The fine sandy beach offered a good landing place and this was always a fishing centre. The smacks from Brixham made their

In many inshore fishing communities the women retailed the catch. These are fishwives at Llangwyn, Pembrokeshire in about 1895   (Welsh Folk Museum)

base here and many men settled locally. A harbour wall was built, but when Milford Haven docks were developed in the late Victorian times this became the main fishing centre of South Wales.

The fishing communities around St Bride's bay, in the very south-west of Wales, were never developed beyond inshore boats. The fishermen of Marloes used to work off the shingle beach in Martin's Haven. It is believed that at its peak in the 1880s around twenty boats worked from Martin's Haven. Much of the lobster-potting took place round Skomer and Skokholm and the fishermen also acted as ferrymen out to both of these islands. In 1871 Skomer had a population of eighteen, but the last permanent resident left just after World War II. Today the island is a nature reserve, and some summers as many as four thousand people take the boat trip from Martin's Haven out to Skomer. The island of Ramsey is reached by a ferry running from St Davids and St Justinian.

The place names on Ramsey are Welsh, but the island's name and that of Skokholm, Skomer and Grassholm are all Scandinavian, an indication that the Vikings were once based in this area. The area has long been English speaking, but this resulted from later settlers.

The three main Pembroke islands were all inhabited into this century. The fourth and smaller island, Grassholm, which was not inhabited, is some ten miles off shore, but in

142

the 1890s the Marloes fishermen rowed out to them to collect birds eggs, mainly gannets, and set lobster pots. The Marloes men mostly fished around Skokholm and if weather turned bad, particularly a fresh north breeze, the boats landed on the Gateholm, a small inshore island. At the eastern end of this was a flat rock where they landed and they then hoisted the boats up on to the Horse Neck. A tackle was carried in the boat especially for this purpose.

The fishermen also went out to the Pembroke islands to kill seals. The skins were sold for waistcoats, belts and bags and the oil was used for farm machinery. There is an account in 1715 of seals being killed with sticks, but this practice died out early in this century when they were shot with rifles. However, the increase in the number of seals naturally meant that they ate more fish and this caused a subsequent decline in the earnings of the fishermen. The Marloes men seem to have been as much hunters as fishermen because they also caught rabbits in the winter on Skomer and Skokholm.

With the decline of the herring in the 1920s, lobstering and crayfishing became the main occupation of fishermen in North Pembroke. The men of Solva, Porthglais and

A boat under repair at Little Haven, Pembrokeshire in 1936   (Welsh Folk Museum)

Porthgain preferred to use Cornish 'inkpot' lobster pots which were made locally of willow and had a single entrance at the top. There were about a dozen different types of lobster pots used between Pembroke and Anglesey and the Welsh Folk Museum at St Fagan near Cardiff has a good collection of these and other fishing gear. This collection was gathered by J. Geraint Jenkins, curator of the Welsh Industrial and Maritime Museum, Cardiff. Dr Jenkins, whose home is at Llangrannog, did the research on herring fishing along the Welsh coast on which this section of the chapter is based.

Many of the men of the villages of Aberporth, Tresaith and Llangrannog were until World War I merchant seamen in the spring and summer and they returned home for the autumn and winter herring fishing. These villages had locally-owned trading ketches and smacks which discharged coal on the open beach in the summer. In 1975 eighty-two year old L. J. Williams of Llangrannog told me about the days when *Margaret Ellen*, *Eliza Jane* and *Albatross* were traders to the village. His explanation of their method of discharge appears in my book *British Sail*. 'Coal was unloaded on the open beach all through the summer, and in the winter they were laid up in the River Teifi, an unusual practice. Their way of getting the coal out was also fairly unusual. A spar was hoisted aloft and a basket in the hold was fixed to the end tilted down. From the high end a rope ran down through a block fixed in the sand and then to a horse. When the horse walked forward the coal-filled basket was brought up to deck level and tipped into a cart at the side. At the same time sand was loaded as ballast for the return passage.'

Mr Williams had actually gone away to sea from the large coal ports of South Wales, but the usual local practice was for the men to get a ship which would return from a voyage at the time the herring fishing started. The Aberporth boats used sail when they

Spritsail rigged boats hauled ashore at Criccieth about 1886   (Gwynedd Archives Service)

144

were after lobster and mackerel, but sails were put ashore when herring started. The practice of just rowing with drift nets seems to have been common in Cardigan Bay. The Aberporth men rowed about six miles down the coast on the ebb to Mwnt and Cardigan Island. About twenty drift nets, each 50ft long were shot across the tide and then the boats drifted back on the flood tide. This method was known as 'drifio' and it was no doubt easier to control the nets under oar than under sail.

The Aberporth boats were between 25–30ft long and for herring drifting had a crew of five to eight men. From the late eighteenth century and during the nineteenth century the Cardigan Bay fishermen used a bluff-bowed boat with a transom stern. This type had all gone from Aberporth beach by 1905 and had been replaced with double-ended boats. Working practices have tended to go round in circles. In mid-Wales and other areas such as the Clyde there was a return to the double-ended hull. Not every 'Norse' hull type in Britain has a clear ancestry back to the Vikings.

The reappearance of the double-ended hull in Cardigan Bay was due to the arrival of the railway turning Aberystwyth into a holiday resort. Taking holiday makers on short sea trips gave a welcome source of summer income to the fishermen. The problem was that the shingle beach was very steep and no landing stages were used. The boats dropped an anchor about thirty yards offshore and then ran straight into the beach. While the passengers were coming aboard on long gang planks over the bows, the sea smashing against the flat transom sterns sometimes threw spray over everybody. This drenching discouraged passengers and in about 1895 the local boatbuilder David Williams overcame the problem by building the 40ft *Victory* with a pointed stern which parted the seas.

This design was such a success that there was a complete swing to double-ended boats at Aberystwyth. The 16–21ft versions of this hull were very popular because two men could go drifting for herring and in the summer hand lining for whiting on the grounds seven miles off Aberystwyth, and they could also take visitors for trips. The 18ft boats were licenced by the town council to carry eight passengers accompanied by one beachman. These boats carried a single dipping lug, but the larger Aberystwyth craft carried three masts on which were set standing sprit sails. This rig was not very good for sailing against the wind and usually they were rowed to windward. When these boats were used for herring drifting the main (central) mast was removed to give more room to work the nets.

The three-masted rig is reputed to have been introduced to Aberystwyth from the neighbouring beach landing of Borth in about 1840. These open three-masters worked the herring shoals anywhere between Newquay and Porthmadog. The rail link with industrial towns inland brought great prosperity to this coast which had previously been isolated behind the Cambrian mountains. One of the sailing pleasure boats was the carvel-built *City of Birmingham*, no doubt named in honour of her patrons. After World War I the pleasure boats were fitted with engines and then were replaced by decked motor boats. The motor boats were too large to be hauled up the beach and were kept in the harbour. The motor boats remained shallow draught under the bow so that they could land on the beach, but their increased length kept their counter sterns clear of the surf. The largest Aberystwyth motor pleasure boat was the 64ft *Worcester Castle*, built for Benjamin White at Appledore in 1926.

At the north end of Cardigan Bay, Lleyn Peninsula juts out into the Irish Sea and forms Caernarfon Bay to the north. Almost on the end of Lleyn is Aberdaron, which, as well as being known as a crab and lobster fishing village, has for centuries been the point of embarkation for people going out to Bardsey Isle. The Aberdaron boats were noted for their excellent sailing qualities. The noted local builder was John Thomas who died in about 1960. At one time he had lived on Bardsey, but later he was building at Aberdaron and Rhiw. Thomas did the whole process of building himself, starting with felling the larch trees and then going on to shaping the planks by hand. Thomas' boats were mostly 12–16ft long. Those with centreboard, jib, mainsail and four oars were called cychod banw (female boat) while the shallow rowing boats were cwch gwrw (male boats).

The northern shore of Lleyn is lined with mountains which often fall sheer into the sea. Between these mountains and cliffs are rocky coves like the one at Porth Ysgaden. This is the beach landing for Tudweiliog, and inland village. At Porth Ysgaden is an old coal wharf and a few boats are kept here by part-time fishermen. However, one man still works regularly through the summer from here, laying pots about five miles along the coast. The lobsters are put in a keep pot and collected once a week by lorry from Caernarfon.

A double ended herring boat at Nefyn, north Wales c.1900   (Gwynedd Archives Service)

Porth Dinllaen is a cove sheltered from the south west by a headland. This is the main beach landing for the little inland town of Nefyn. In medieval times herring fishing was practised here as a supplementary occupation to pastoral farming. In 1635 most of the men in Nefyn were fishermen. By the nineteenth century a small pier under Nefyn Point gave protection to about forty boats and by this time there were mackerel, herring and lobster fishermen and others which were part time quarrymen and merchant sailors. There were also shipbuilding yards at Nefyn. Between the launching of the sloop *Hopewell* in 1760 and the schooner *Venus* in 1880, 185 ships were built at Nefyn. Mostly these were tubby little brigs of about 80ft long, but three larger barques were built here. This was not unusual, for in Caernarvonshire, the north part of the modern county of Gwynedd, between 1759–1913 1,149 vessels were built, mostly in ports with harbours; but five were built at Aberdaron, three at Rhiw and another three at Llanbedrog. Most of the wooden local traders were engaged in taking goods, often off open beaches, to Liverpool. This included barrels of herring, but between 1840-60 slate was the main trade for these vessels.

In 1910 Nefyn still had forty herring boats which were manned in the season by three or four men. The boats were double-ended to allow for easier launching, although Nefyn's gently sloping sandy beach, with only a slight tide rise and fall, was regarded as being a safe landing.

It was believed that herring came close inshore on a new moon and stayed further out during dark nights. Fine one-inch mesh nets were usually purchased from Bridport or East Anglia for fishing. The nets were anchored in lines to the bottom and inspected every day just before dawn. About every six days the nets were hauled and reset. The fishermen of Aberdaron also anchored their herring nets down tide because the currents were too strong to allow them to drift freely. Nets could only be anchored safely in certain areas and there was an unwritten law which said where each village's grounds were.

The fishermen of Aberdaron came up the coast and lodged their boats at Porth Dinllaen for part of the Nefyn season. The Lleyn spawning herring were known as soldiers and there was little demand for them while the Nefyn herring were recognised as being better. These were described as

Penwaig Nefyn, penwaig Nefyn   (Nefyn herring, Nefyn herring)
Bolin fel tafarnwyr   (Bellies like innkeepers)
Cefna' fel ffarmwrs   (Backs like farmers)

In Lleyn and Nefyn most of the herrings were bought by travelling salesmen, but at Moelfre, Anglesey's leading beach landing, boys were sent to walk round the district selling herring from door to door. The most prolific Anglesey herring grounds were off the east coast. At Moelfre, nets were anchored and then on the daily haul were pulled across the boats and reshot on the other side.

The Moelfre men used to go off the beach at 4.30 a.m. and it is said that the local pubs sold more beer before 4.30 a.m. than during the rest of the day. The herring petered out here in the early 1930s when local stocks were exhausted. Men then had to seek other employment. Dick Evans went away in coastal merchant ships, but returned to lobster potting off the beach. He also became coxswain of the Moelfre lifeboat and in this work became one of the most decorated coxswains in the Royal National Lifeboat Institution.

By the 1970s the pub at Moelfre had been restyled to catch the eye of passing tourists. The winches were still on the tiny beach of grey pebbles, but only a few pleasure boats are there now. There are two pot boats though operating off an incredibly small patch of shingle in the cliff foot near the old lifeboat shed.

Also on the east coast of Anglesey is Bull Bay, which is just a cleft in the low cliff. This was also once an important herring landing beach in the season between October and February. But that has all gone long ago and the slipway down to the water is used by one boat for potting and a mass of pleasure craft now fill the old boat place across the road.

Rhosneigr on the west coast of Anglesey appears to have once been a beach landing, although it is now a holiday village. To reach the beach, craft must come in through a narrow channel in a mass of rocks. Boats, including several used for potting, lie on moorings which dry out. One pot boat lies on a mooring in a reef which seems very exposed, with the seas pounding over the reef. Every summer sees some pleasure boats breaking loose and hammering to pieces on the hard sandy beach.

On the mainland of Gwynedd the best known inshore fishery is the mussel-gathering in the Conwy estuary which is undertaking by members of four families. Just to the west of the estuary in Conwy Bay is a pier at Penmaenmawr which is one of the few places left where commercial ships load off an open beach. The 'Pen' pier in Conwy Bay is sheltered to a certain extent by eastern Anglesey and Great Ormes Head. In the sailing ship days two piers were built in Conwy Bay to load 'sets' (street paving stones) but only the Pen pier remains. This was enlarged when steamers were introduced by building another pier over the top of the original structure. After World War II the Penmaenmawr Quarry was exporting granite chips for road works to Hamburg. Ships of up to 1500 tons came into the pier, remained afloat and were loaded in the two hours either side of high water. This trade ceased in about 1978 when the pier was found to be in need of repair but the owners, Kingston Minerals, intend to open it again.

The Quarry at Llanddulas also has a pier, but this section of the North Wales coast has no beach landings. In fact the whole of this coast from Anglesey up to the Solway Firth has few beach boats which are daily hauled out of the water, but between the River Dee and Morecambe there are many places where boats are kept on moorings off open beaches. Fishing on the River Dee was once a full time occupation. To conserve salmon stocks the Dee and Clwyd River Athority only issue netting licences to a few men. A fisherman netting between March 1 and August 31 usually lands about 70–100 salmon.

Most of the Dee salmon boats are kept at Handbridge, a part of Chester and the limit of the tidal Dee. The boats used are about 17ft long, clinker built with wide sterns from which the 'draft net' is shot while the boat is rowed in a circle from the bank. Both ends of the net are then hauled to the bank to form a bag. In the lower Dee, where the tide runs hard, a drift trammel net is used. The actual fishing is done under oar although an outboard is used to reach the spot chosen. In the pre-engine days the Dee salmon boats set a simple, but effective spritsail. This sail could be stowed up against the mast by lowering the sprit to avoid taking up precious working space in the boat.

In 1982 there were seven traditional stern deck salmon boats at Handbridge as well as

148

The nobby *Enid*, built at Arnside in 1936, boiling shrimps off Hoylake, 1982 (Author)

a few modern hulls fitted out for salmon netting. Most of the traditional salmon boats had been built at Taylor's, a boatyard at the seaward lock in the Shropshire Union Canal. The Manifold family, who have been fishing on the Dee for over two hundred years, had their boat the *Margaret* built by Arthur Taylor in 1923. In 1979 seventy-three year old Arthur Taylor, who had not built a salmon boat for twenty years, got out his old patterns and in some 500 man hours built the 17ft 6in salmon boat *Arthur*. She was built for the Merseyside Maritime Museum who also have the 17ft 6in *Joan*, built by Arthur Taylor in 1946. Another salmon boat was built for Chester Museum and is now on display, with a workshop from Taylor's Yard at Ellesmere Port Canal Museum.

The Dee salmon fishing is certainly very ancient and was well organised and controlled in medieval times. The methods have not altered a great deal over the centuries, nor have many of the families involved. The Bithells of Flint have been fishing on the Dee for over three hundred years. The methods and boats used in this fishery are a careful balance between conserving stocks and allowing a limited number of men to earn a reasonable return from it.

On the Wirral peninsula, facing Liverpool Bay, is Hoylake where a few fishing boats and yachts lie on moorings off the open coast, with a landing on a concrete slipway. The Hoylake is a corruption of the original High Lake referring to a deep pool in the sands. This was an important fishing centre before the Port of Liverpool developed. Up to

149

World War I most of the Liverpool trawling smacks were owned and crewed by Hoylake men. In 1982 there were three boats shrimping from Hoylake, mainly on the East Hoyle Bank. Some of the shrimps were retailed to the public on the landing slip and others sold to local shops. One place famed for the sale of shrimps on the Wirral is Parkgate. In 1900 there were still shrimpers working from Parkgate, but the Dee has now silted up so that the waterfront faces a vast expanse of marsh which is seldom covered by water. Parkgate had been an Irish packet ship port and a fashionable resort in the eighteenth century, then a resort and boat landing in the nineteenth century but now it is a seaside resort without the sea.

From Hoylake north to Morecambe Bay is truly the shrimp coast. The shrimp (locally called prawns) thrive in the shallow sea with its sandy bottom. Just before 1900 local men began to exploit this resource with great vigour so that by 1904 Southport and the adjoining coastal resort Marshside had a fleet of about seventy 'nobbies' nearly all less than six years old.

Across the river Ribble at Lytham was another group of shrimp trawlers. These had slightly round bottoms to help take the heavy pounding when the tide ebbed away across the hard sand. The boom in shrimping did not survive World War I, but this fishery has carried on in a small way.

At Southport the shifting sand is pushing the sea further away. To the north, on the nine miles of golden sandy beach on the Flyde peninsula, the cheerful, brash resort of Blackpool grew up as a playground for people in the Lancashire mill towns. During the 'wakes' weeks when the inland mill towns shut down in turn, thousands of people flocked to Blackpool and a trip in a sailing boat was part of the attractions on offer. After 1890 William Stoba, a master shipwright at Fleetwood, designed the sailing pleasure boat which worked off the central beach, Blackpool. In 1980 Blackpool had six million staying visitors and twenty million day trippers. Trips in motor launches off the beach are still part of the numerous attractions of Blackpool and in the winter these launches are stored on the seafront waiting for the crowds to return.

Morecambe is the most northerly of the Lancashire holiday resorts and before World War I seems to have concentrated on sailing pleasure boats as a means of giving trippers some form of entertainment. During the summer over a hundred men were working on the pleasure boats from seven piers on Morecambe seafront. In 1900 there were thirty-two sailing boats, all fine lined half decked gaff cutters of nobby type, operated by six companies and 158 rowing boats which were hired out. There were also sailing fishing boats which as early as the 1840s were racing in the Morecambe Fishermen's regattas. These sailing boats, mostly built by Crossfield of Arnside, who developed the 'nobby' type, were gaff cutters specially evolved to beat to windward in the narrow channels of Morecambe Bay. These cutters were sometimes called prawners, a slightly misleading title since it is shrimps that live on the sand and mud of Morecambe Bay, while the true prawns prefer a rocky seabed.

The 'nobbies' with tanned gaff sails returning to Morecambe with the steam blowing down wind from the shrimp boilers, was one of the sights of the Lancashire coast. As well as shrimps, these trawlers were landing flat fish, particularly Dover Sole. In 1902 there were 115 fishing boats at Morecambe, but many were the open mussel boats which the men worked in the winter on the 'skears' (rocky outcrops) where the mussels

150

gathered. The Morecambe mussel boats were about 16ft long, beamy and flat bottomed so that they could carry a lot of weight. The mussel boats were clinker built and transom sterned, and sailed with a standing lug and sometimes a small foresail. Some had centreboards, which were very unusual in British sailing work boats. The Morecambe men were rather progressive in their outlook, probably because there were no long-standing traditions to break down.

About the time of World War I the fishermen were having a lean time because they were competing against each other to sell fish. In 1919 a fishermen's co-operative was started to market the catch. The fish merchants at the time said that the co-op would only last a fortnight, as the men would fall out amongst themselves. In fact the twelve trawlers still working from Morecambe in 1983 were still selling through this Morecambe Trawler Association, which was by then believed to be the oldest fishermen's selling co-operative in Britain. Some of these boats were modern craft, but others were 'nobbies' like the 35ft *Nance* and the *Maud Raby*, built in 1932. Indeed motorized 'nobbies' are a common sight still on the coast between Hoylake and Maryport.

Morecambe's rise as a resort and fishing centre was due to the rail link with the mill towns of Lancashire and the town quickly overshadowed the older fishing centre of Sunderland Point at the entrance of the River Lune. Sunderland Point, a lonely hamlet half way between Morecambe and Fleetwood, is a microcosm of ancient fishing methods. About 1979 a really high tide, swollen with fresh water after prolonged heavy

High water at Central Beach, Blackpool with tripper boats leaving in about 1900   (Blackpool Library)

Morecambe fishermen gathering mussels with hand forks and then washing them in 'tierniels' (baskets) on 'skears' (beds) left exposed by the ebb tide. This was the normal way to collect mussels, but in this case it was a transplantation exercise organised by the Lancashire and Western Sea Fisheries in about 1904, to try and improve the fishery by starting new beds   (K. Willacy)

rain, washed away part of the saltings in the River Lune just above Sunderland Point, revealing an old fish trap of which no one had any memory. This trap was a wattle fence across a sandbank made to drive the fish into a pocket; the fish were collected at low water. This type of trap was widely used in the medieval period, and most had been abandoned by the end of the nineteenth century, although a similar trap at Cockerham, just outside the Lune, was operated until about 1965. In southern England a fish trap was often called a 'kettle' (hence the old saying 'a pretty kettle of fish'), but on the Lancashire coast they were known as 'bauks'.

The next step on from a bauk was a stake net. This was a net hung between posts on the sands and Sunderland Point fishermen say that the trick was to be there as the tide ebbed to collect the fish before the seagulls started to feed on the fish in the nets. Another form of fish trap is the stownet, a kind of large bag net lowered into the water. These were also of medieval origin and before World War II this method was widely used from anchored boats in Essex, the Solent and the Bristol Channel. At Sunderland Point, small stownets left anchored to the bottom are still in use.

About thirty men used to find employment gathering mussels from Sunderland Point every winter. Often boats sailed over to Glasson Dock carrying a ton of mussels which were sent by rail to the north-east of England for longline bait. In about 1952 the mussel

152

'skears' suddenly died out and the fishery collapsed. This just left the Smith and Gardner families who salmon fished between April and August, went shrimping in the autumn and caught whitebait and sprat in the winter.

The salmon fishermen of Sunderland Point still use open sailing boats because they do not have to travel any distance to use a whammel net, (actually three connecting nets 320 yards long) to drift for salmon. These nets work best in fast tide streams off the mouth of the River Lune in bad weather so a robust boat is needed. The sailing and motor whammel boats are totally different. In about 1965 a double-ended boat was brought over from the north east of England and as it proved popular a mould was taken off at Overton and a GRP motor whammel boat class was started. The older sailing whammel boats are finer lined that the Morecambe mussel boats, but most have clinker hulls and transom sterns except the Gardner's whammel boat *Ivanhoe*, built in 1906, which has a pointed stern. Woodhouse of Overton built most of these boats. The fastest under sail is Tom Smith's *Mary*, built in 1937. She is an open transom sterned clinker boat with no centreboard but will turn to windward over an ebb tide in the Lune.

Some Sunderland Point men just fish between April and August when they hold licences to fish salmon. Harold Gardner is Lune Pilot and his brother Tom skippers the pilot boat. With shipping into Glasson Dock in 1982 at a record level, they had limited

Mussel boats returning to Morecambe to unload into horse carts. The mussels were then taken to the promenade, riddled, cleaned and bagged ready for sending out by train. A nobby is getting under way in the background, c.1895   (K. Willacy)

153

time for fishing. The Smith brothers still fish, but Tom Smith turns his hand to everything, including retailing fish, in order to make it a full time occupation. He also keeps a horse and appears to be the last person to be sand fishing by horse and cart.

The main sand fishing centre is Flookburgh, a rural village a mile inland from the Cartmel Sands at the head of Morecambe Bay. By 1964 tractors towing a trailer and two trawls had been introduced. To call it a beach landing might be stretching a point for at the bottom of the lane the tractor tyre marks fan out across the sands. The tractors are fitted with enlarged mudguards and other shields to protect the engine from salt water spray. The men go out trawling in groups so that if one of the tractors gets stuck, the others can pull it clear. If this fails then the tractor is hurriedly stripped as it sinks into the sand. The horses could not cover so much ground in a tide, but if they hit a soft patch then they instinctively walked faster to avoid sinking in.

The shrimp and flat fish caught on the sands are sold from several houses in Flookburgh. The village is also one of the centres of the autumn cockling and this was also done at Baycliff, Bardsea, Cark and Allithwaite. Just near Allithwaite is the Kent Bank, the starting point at low tide for a twelve mile route across the sands to Hest Bank. This short cut was used by the stage coach to Lancaster and is now walked by thousands of tourists each summer. Next to Kent Bank is Grange-Over-Sands, a pleasant holiday resort which most of the day faces an expanse of sand stretching to the seaward horizon, but the flood tide approaches at an astonishing speed. Between about 1880 and

The Woodhouse's Yard at Overton, where most of the whammel boats were built, c.1910 (Lancaster City Museum)

154

Whammel boats getting under way on the River Lune at Sunderland Point. These boats are setting a standing lug which was a development of the dipping lug   (P. Gilchrist)

the early 1900s pleasure steamers brought visitors from Morecambe who then travelled up to the Lake District. Grange also had a sailing yacht taking trips daily and other tripper boats sailed up on the tide with holiday makers from Morecambe.

The north shore of Morecambe Bay is part of Cumbria. This county is unique in Britain because it has no real beach landings on its coast. The Isle of Man, out in the Irish Sea, has few real beach landings now, but before the construction of harbours the whole Manx economy was based on beach-based fishing. Man was colonized by the Vikings in the ninth and tenth centuries and the Norse type of boat remained standard until the late eighteenth century. These Manx 'scowte' were double-ended clinker craft with single square sails and were used mainly for herring drifting. A smaller type, again double-ended, was the Manx 'baulk' yawl (longline boat).

The Manx 'scowtes' were sometimes called 'squaresails' and were about 20ft long and carried a crew of five. The drift nets were 40 fathoms long and were made in the long winter evenings from wool produced by the Manx sheep. The Manx men were fishermen-crofters and their whole life style was rather similar to that of the men in Shetland. Until about 1790 all fish caught were used for local consumption. The herring caught in the season between May and September were either eaten fresh or salted down in barrels for the winter.

The Manx economy was revolutionized by the export of fish which started in 1790. The men abandoned the simple double-ender for off-shore work and switched to 30ft

155

gaff cutters, and in the 1830s they adopted the 40ft dandies which were two-masted luggers. A fleet of eighty-six dandies belonged to the various Manx fishing harbours. The herring was proving something of a bonanza with some of the boats earning £1000 in a season which was about twice the value of the new boats.

In about 1870 the island builder started to build a new faster and slightly larger type of lugger called a nickey. These were modelled on the Cornish drifters which visited the island. Since many of the Cornish men were called Nicholas, this type was called 'nickey'. About a decade later another Manx lugger appeared called the 'nobby', which had a standing lugsail on the foremast. At its peak in around the 1890s, the Manx fleet comprised 120 boats at Port St Mary, 250 at Peel and about 50 between Ramsey and Laxey. There were a few more at Douglas although this ferry port was already relying on the tourist industry with visitors from Lancashire's industrial towns. The Manx owners did not venture into steam drifters and the fishing fleet gradually melted away in the opening decades of this century.

The main fishing grounds were to the south of Man, so many of the luggers were owned in Port St Mary which had a harbour; but they also operated from Port Erin which is a mile away by land and has a bay sheltered by the high ground of Bradda Head. A stone pier was built to protect craft lying on the beach. Long after the herring fleet had gone, Port Erin boatmen turned to the new industry of tourism by running boat trips to the bird sanctuary on the Calf of Man.

Port Erin is on the southern end of Man and on the island's west coast. North of here the coast is mainly cliffs but there are some old thatched fishermen's cottages in the lovely bay at Niarbyl. The north end of Man is flat and has many Norse place names. It was here on Lhen shore that the last baulk yawl worked until the 1930s. These yawls retained the double-ended clinker hulls which suggest a Norse origin. Certainly the name baulk yawl came from the Scandinavian 'baak' for longline.

Back from the northern plain the land rises to the summit of Snaefell from where on a fine day England, Scotland, Wales and Ireland can all be seen. The British Isles can be divided up into all kinds of political and cultural groups, but the history of small working craft underlines their common ancestry. From this common ancestry the beach boats branched out into many local types, reaching a peak at the Victorian period. The beach boats of Britain may be a link with an age before the industrial revolution, but they also give an income to the men who work them today.

Bibliography

Bouquet, Michael   *South Eastern Sail* (David & Charles 1972)
Gillis, R. H. C.   *Pilot Gigs of Cornwall & the Isles of Scilly* (Isles of Scilly Museum)
Green, Charles   *Sutton Hoo* (Merlin Press 1963)
Hill, Oliver H.   *The English Coble* (National Maritime Museum 1978)
Hornell, James   *The Fishing Luggers of Hastings* (Society for Nautical Research)
Hutchings, Richard J.   *Island Longshoremen* (G. G. Saunders 1975)
Jenkins, A. J.   *Gigs and Cutters of the Isles of Scilly* (Isles of Scilly Gig Racing Committee 1975)
Jenkins, J. Geraint   *Boat House and Net House* (National Museum of Wales)
Leather, John   *Spritsails and Lugsails* (Granada Publishing 1979)
Magnusson, Magnus   *Vikings* (Bodley Head 1980)
Malster, Robert   *Lowestoft, East Coast Port* (Terence Dalton 1982)
Nicholson, J. R.   *Shetlands Fishing Vessels* (Shetland Times 1981)
Old Gaffers Association (compiled by John Scarlett) *Register of Gaff Rigged Boats* (Old Gaffers Association 1981)
Simper, Robert   *Britain's Maritime Heritage* (David & Charles 1982)
Simper, Robert   *British Sail* (David & Charles 1977)
Simper, Robert   *East Coast Sail* (David & Charles 1972)
Simper, Robert   *Traditions of East Anglia* (Boydell Press 1980)
Stibbons, Peter, Katherine Lee, Martin Warren   *Crabs & Shannocks* (Poppyland Publishing, Cromer 1983)
Willmott, F. G.   *Bricks & Brickies* (F. G. Willmott 1972)

Periodicals
Cornish Life, Belmont House, Redruth, TR15 1JZ
Fishing News, Heighway House, 87 Blackfriars Road, London SE1 8HB
Flouwin' Tide, Scottish Veteran & Vintage Fishing Vessel Club, St Ayles, Anstruther, Fife KY10 3AB
Motor Boat & Yachting, Dorset House, Stamford Street, London SE1
Northern Studies
Sea Breezes, The Magazine of Ships & the Sea, 202 Cotton Building, Old Hall Street, Liverpool L3 9LA
Ulster Folk Life, The Ulster Folk & Transport Museum, Holywood, Co Down, Ulster
Wooden Boat, P.O. Box 78, Brooklin ME USA.

Index

158